TACITUS' *Agricola, Germany,* AND *Dialogue on Orators*

OKLAHOMA SERIES IN CLASSICAL CULTURE

Oklahoma Series in Classical Culture

Series Editor

A. J. Heisserer, University of Oklahoma

Advisory Board

TACITUS' *Agricola,*
Germany AND
Dialogue on Orators

Revised Edition

Translated, with an Introduction and
Notes, by **Herbert W. Benario**

UNIVERSITY OF OKLAHOMA PRESS : NORMAN AND LONDON

By Herbert W. Benario

Tacitus: Agricola, Germany, Dialogue on Orators (trans. and ed.) (Indianapolis, 1967)
An Introduction to Tacitus (Athens, Ga., 1975)
A Commentary on the Vita Hadriani in the Historia Augusta (Decatur, Ga., 1980)
Tacitus Annals 11 and 12 (Lanham, Md., 1983)
Basil Lanneau Gildersleeve: An American Classicist (coed.) (Baltimore, 1986)
The Classical Association of the Middle West and South: A History of the First Eighty Years (Greenville, S.C., 1989)
Caesaris Augusti Res Gestae et Fragmenta (Detroit, Mich., 1990)
Tacitus' Agricola, Germany, and Dialogue on Orators, rev. ed. (Norman, 1991)

Library of Congress Cataloging-in-Publication Data

Tacitus, Cornelius.
    [Selections. English. 1991]
    Tacitus' Agricola, Germany, and Dialogue on orators / translated, with an introduction and notes, by Herbert W. Benario. — Rev. ed.
      p. cm. — (Oklahoma series in classical culture; v. 8)
    Rev. ed. of: Agricola, Germany, Dialogue on orators. 1967.
    Includes bibliographical references and index.
    ISBN 0-8061-2321-4 (alk. paper)
    1. Tacitus, Cornelius—Translations, English. 2. Agricola, Gnaeus Julius, 40–93. 3. Great Britain—History—Roman period, 55 B.C.–449 A.D. 4. Germany—History—To 843. 5. Statesmen—Rome—Biography. 6. Oratory, Ancient. I. Benario, Herbert W. II. Tacitus, Cornelius. Agricola, Germany, Dialogue on orators. III. Title. IV. Title: Agricola, Germany, and Dialogue on orators. V. Series.
PA6707.A7B4   1991
878'.0109—dc20
                                     90-48807
                                        CIP

The paper in this book meets the guidelines for permanence and durability of the Committee on Production Guidelines for Book Longevity of the Council of Library Resources, Inc.

Tacitus' Agricola, Germany, and Dialogue on Orators is Volume 8 in the Oklahoma Series in Classical Culture.

Contents

Maps

Preface to the Revised Edition

Some reviewers of the first edition took offense at the peculiarity of the English translation in some passages. Although I recognize the validity of their response, I have not chosen to alter my version, save occasionally when I have had second thoughts, certainly an expected result of more than twenty years of further reading and study of Tacitus. The choices that a translator makes regarding his purpose will never satisfy all readers. Let me give an example.

In 1965 the Bobbs-Merrill Company published a volume, *Roman Drama*, with translations by Frank O. Copley of the plays of Plautus and Terence and by Moses Hadas of the plays of Seneca. Copley wrote that he had "attempted to translate ideas and situations rather than words. I kept one question constantly before me: If this character were speaking contemporary American English, how would he have expressed the idea he has in mind? It will be immediately obvious that this principle is bound, on occasion, to lead to an English version that bears little resemblance, on the purely verbal level, to the original Latin." Hadas, on the other hand, chose not "to make Seneca a contemporary but . . . to reflect his own rhetorical virtuosity in vocabulary and syntax. Rhetoric is as important in Senecan tragedy as music is in operatic libretto, and to efface it would strip the plays of what makes them moving and meaningful, and leave only a bare framework of frightfulness."

I preferred the model of Hadas, and still think that is the proper approach to Tacitus. His style is rhetorical and brilliant, vastly different from that of Cicero except in the *Dialogue on Orators*. A translation of Cicero will, and should, read like good English, familiar to those who know Gibbon and Churchill. I did not want Tacitus to seem like Cicero to a modern reader; his style was unquestionably hard for his contemporaries, and it should not be made bland in another language. If my English is occasionally awkward, in a passage where the Latin is awkward, I shall be satisfied.

The texts now used are the latest Teubner editions, all published in Stuttgart in 1983: J. Delz, *Agricola;* A. Önnerfors, *Germania;* and H. Heubner, *Dialogus de Oratoribus.* Commentaries which appeared after the first edition and have occasionally been useful in revision are R. M. Ogilvie and I. Richmond, *Cornelii Taciti de Vita Agricolae* (Oxford, 1967); R. Much, *Die Germania des Tacitus*, third edition by H. Jankuhn and W. Lange (Heidelberg, 1967); R. Güngerich, *Kommentar zum Dialogus des Tacitus* (Göttingen, 1980); and H. Heubner, *Kommentar zum Agricola des Tacitus* (Göttingen, 1984).

I am grateful to the University of Oklahoma Press's anonymous readers for their comments and suggestions which have led to amendment and improvement.

H. W. B.

Preface to the First Edition

For a translator to speak of the nature of his version even before the reader has had the opportunity to scan the first page of it may seem inappropriate. Yet it appears to me not only proper but necessary for a translator of Tacitus to explain the ground rules he has followed. Tacitus' Latin is often so concise and contorted that many think it an impossibility to translate him, and are content to settle for paraphrase or a sprightly modern version. I have tried to translate Tacitus faithfully, as I understand and interpret him, in language as well as idea. I have not sought to produce a text stripped of all peculiarities of style; I have sought to give a sense of Tacitus' rhetoric, his choice of parts of speech, his sentence connections and absence of them, and other individual traits. For without them we do not acquire much taste of Tacitus' unique qualities.

The text followed here is the 1957 Teubner edition of E. Koestermann. The very few places where I have departed from his readings are indicated in footnotes. I have drawn upon the rich stores of various commentaries: H. Furneaux and J. G. C. Anderson's *De Vita Agricolae* and Anderson's *De Origine et Situ Germanorum* (Oxford: Clarendon Press, 1922 and 1938), G. Forni's editions of the two (Rome: Edizioni dell'Ateneo, 1962 and 1964), A. Gudeman's *Dialogus de oratoribus* (Boston: Allyn and Bacon, 1898), and W. Peterson's *Dialogus de oratoribus* (Oxford: Oxford University Press, 1893). As always, good commentaries make a translator's task easier. I have also had at my side the translations of A. J. Church and W. J. Brodribb, *The Complete Works of Tacitus* (New York: Modern Library, edited by M. Hadas, 1942); H. Mattingly, *Tacitus on Britain and Germany* (Baltimore: Penguin Classics, 1948); W. Peterson, *The Dialogue on Oratory* (London and New York: Loeb Classical Library, 1920); and K. Büchner, *Tacitus: Die historischen Versuche*, second edition (Stuttgart: Kröner, 1963).

My colleagues, Professors Douglas J. Stewart and Joseph M. Conant, have placed me in their debt by their willingness to read parts of the manuscript and make suggestions for improvement. I have profited greatly from their comments, particularly those of Professor Stewart, who will recognize in the final version many passages that are the better for his incisive criticism. Mrs. Martha F. McKay, secretary of the Department of Classics, Emory

University, has typed the manuscript in her customary, impeccable manner; I am grateful for service beyond the call of duty. But my wife has had to live with this work from its genesis, and by suggestion and endurance she has helped enormously. I therefore dedicate it to her with affection and love, *parvum pro multo*.

HERBERT W. BENARIO

TACITUS' *Agricola, Germany,* AND *Dialogue on Orators*

Introduction

Publius Cornelius Tacitus, Rome's greatest historian, was born about A.D. 55, perhaps in northern Italy or southern France. His birth thus coincides approximately with the accession of Nero as emperor; the deposition and subsequent suicide of the latter brought about the first great crisis of succession in the empire, which was to be settled by arms. That long year, 68–69, impressed itself vividly upon the mind of the young Tacitus; neither Rome nor the provinces were spared the cataclysmic consequences of that upheaval.

The ultimate triumph of Vespasian ushered in a new era; Tacitus entered upon a public career in the capital. The details of his advancement are known; he held minor offices under Vespasian, attained the quaestorship in the early eighties, and the double distinction of a praetorship and a priesthood in 88, when Domitian was in the eighth year of his reign. The ancient republican colleges of priests retained their prestige under the principate, and his designation as *quindecimvir sacris faciundis*, a member of the board of fifteen charged with the supervision of certain religious ceremonies, was a particular honor in this year, when Domitian celebrated the secular games, the *ludi saeculares*, for which, on another occasion, several generations earlier, Horace had composed a splendid hymn.

The years 89–93 were spent away from Rome, either in service as a legionary commander or as governor of a minor province; both were likely stages in a promising senatorial career. These were years in which it was good to be away from Rome; Domitian's autocratic nature hardened after a challenge to his position in 89, and the dark days of a reign of terror, with the extinction of many of the best of the senatorial class, ensued.

Upon his return to Rome, Tacitus shared the brooding despondency of his peers until a new dawn arose in 96 with the assassination of Domitian. An elderly senator, Marcus Cocceius Nerva, succeeded, but his position was insecure because of the grumblings of the praetorian guard over the murder of Domitian and because of his lack of prestige with the armies on the frontiers. In 97, Nerva adopted as his colleague and destined successor the outstanding general of Rome's armies, who was then governor in Germany. The choice of Marcus Ulpius Traianus, known to posterity as Trajan, was singularly felicitous; it was the key event in the chain of events responsible for the period of the five good emperors, the happiest period of man's history, as Gibbon noted.

It seems unquestionable that Nerva's decision to attach Trajan to his support resulted from internal power politics which might well have exploded into a civil war comparable to that of almost thirty years before. It is intriguing to speculate upon the role played by the consuls of that year, particularly because Tacitus was one of the suffect consuls late in the year. (Under the principate, the consuls who held office at the beginning of the year were known as *ordinarii;* their names designated the year. They were normally succeeded by *consules suffecti.* There was no specified length of time any of the consuls held office, but four months was a popular term.)

Tacitus had various official posts open to him as an ex-consul, but we do not know whether he held any government office for some fifteen years following. In the year 100 he was appointed counsel, together with Pliny the Younger, for the people of the province of Africa, in a suit for extortion and general malfeasance in office against their former governor, Marius Priscus. Pliny led off for the prosecution and spoke for five hours without a break. Tacitus summed up the case; his address was most eloquent and marked with the majesty characteristic of his manner of speech. The prosecution was victorious; the consul designate, who was the first to express his opinion before the senate, added that the counselors had performed their duty well, in a manner worthy of the charge laid upon them.

Tacitus was now at the height of his power and renown as an orator, yet he seems never to have delivered another speech. His friend Pliny's long and involved, often turgid, address of gratitude to the emperor upon his entry to the office of consul in September 100, the *Panegyricus,* may have convinced Tacitus that the day of meaningful oratory, in a style congenial to him, had long since passed.

For the rest of his life, he devoted himself to historiography, interrupted only by his tenure of the governorship of the province of Asia in 112–113, one of the two most important provinces under the senate's jurisdiction. It was the climax of a public career for a senator. We do not know when Tacitus died; it seems certain that he survived Trajan. The telling question, which can only be answered with hypotheses, is how much of the reign of

Hadrian he saw. The date of his demise is variously given as early as 117 or as late as about 130.

The career of Tacitus the statesman cannot, and should not, be separated from the writings of Tacitus the historian. A point that has been recently well emphasized is that in antiquity the writing of history is generally the sphere of a man who has participated in the making of it, for only thus could he gain insight into the interrelationships of events and the workings of men's minds. So it was with Thucydides, Polybius, Cato, and Sallust. Tacitus, among the Romans, is certainly the supreme example of the effect of personal experience upon historical outlook. One must not forget that he was a senator before he became an historian.

Although Pliny's loquaciousness is often boring, it is his sometimes naïve delight with life and people, expressed in his letters, which enables us to discern some of Tacitus' personal qualities. Pliny was some half-dozen years Tacitus' junior and looked up to him with admiration and a certain awe. Their political careers were very similar, although Pliny reached the consulship seven years after his praetorship, whereas it took Tacitus nine. The rapidity suggests special favor with the emperor. Pliny's last public office was as imperial legate of the province of Bithynia, perhaps in the very years during which Tacitus served in Asia, with the particular charge of unraveling the province's financial affairs.

Pliny addressed eleven letters to Tacitus and speaks of him in three others. There are instances of good-natured banter and the frank comments and criticisms of close friends: Pliny tells Tacitus that he took his writing tablets along on a hunting trip, and says that Tacitus should not laugh at this (1.6). Pliny, in a long letter, argues that speeches should be lengthy and full rather than brief, but he is willing to be dissuaded by Tacitus (1.20). We can, I think, envision a smile on Tacitus' face as he, the master of Latin brevity and the pungent epigram, read this plea for the other side. Pliny requests Tacitus' assistance in obtaining teachers for a new school at Comum, Pliny's home town, which he is helping to endow (4.13); he responds affirmatively to Tacitus' request that he support the candidature of a young man for public office (6.9); he speaks feelingly of the close rapport between them and asserts Tacitus' preeminence in oratory (7.20), and acknowledges a speech that Tacitus has sent him for criticism (8.7). Pliny complains about his inability to do serious work while he is on vacation in the country (9.10). He exhorts Tacitus that they should both continue their writing as they have begun (9.14), for it has brought them both fame, and, what is even better, their names are always joined. He delights in telling Maximus an anecdote Tacitus had told him: Tacitus was sitting in a theater when a stranger nearby asked him whether he came from Rome or a province; Tacitus replied that the man should know him from his writings; he then asked, "Are you Tacitus or Pliny?" (9.23). In another letter, to Minicius Fundanus, Pliny speaks of Tacitus, saying with admiration, "You know what kind of man he is" (4.15).

Three letters are addressed to Tacitus the historian rather than Tacitus the man and friend. Of these, two are long and detailed descriptions of the eruption of Vesuvius, written in response to Tacitus' request for such information to be used in his *Histories*. Pliny tells, in the first, of the actions and ultimate death of his uncle, the elder Pliny, who commanded the fleet stationed in the Bay of Naples; in the other he relates the experiences shared by himself and his mother (6.16 and 20). In the last Pliny hopes that a bit of immortality may be given him by having his role in the prosecution of Baebius Massa, a notorious case in the year 93, which brought Pliny considerable renown, included in Tacitus' work; he therefore gives Tacitus the details. For, he says, he is convinced that Tacitus' history will be immortal: *Auguror, nec me fallit augurium, historias tuas immortales futuras* ("I prophesy, and I am not wrong in my prophecy, that your histories will be immortal") (7.33).

Tacitus was the author of five works; three are brief, independent monographs, two are long, detailed, closely related narratives. The first and earliest is the *Agricola*, a eulogistic biography of his father-in-law, which appeared early in 98. Tacitus was then in his early forties; the fresh air of the reign of Nerva and Trajan had begun to efface some of the bitter memories of the terrible days under Domitian, when it was dangerous to think what one wished and to say what one thought. Tacitus, unlike some others, not only had survived that period but had experienced no obstacle in his public career. His temperament was clearly not that of a martyr who dies flamboyantly but without any worthwhile accomplishment—men like himself, after all, were needed to keep the empire functioning—but he may have felt a pang of conscience that he had not outwardly opposed Domitian. Neither had Agricola, who had served Rome well, nor had Trajan, who had reached the consulship in 91 and had later been entrusted with the command of Rome's most important armies. It may be that we can discern a bit of the quality of an *apologia pro vita sua* in Tacitus' statement at the end of chapter 42 about those who are faithful servants of government.

The publication of the *Agricola* was followed almost immediately by that of the *Germany*, an ethnographical treatise, as it seems best understood, which may indeed have had its genesis in the preceding year. Whether Tacitus had an ulterior motive in writing this work is a question that cannot be answered with any certainty. Many scholars think that it contains veiled advice, or even a warning, for the newly destined emperor, Trajan, who was then resident on the Rhine frontier, by underscoring the great threat to Rome from the Germans and suggesting that they were Rome's greatest potential danger. Coincidentally, he could belittle Domitian's claim to have pacified Germany. If this was Tacitus' purpose, it had no success, for Trajan preferred to retain the *status quo* in Germany and even echo Domitian's boast in his first minting, by issuing coins with the legend *Germania pacata* ("Germany pacified"). The emperor thought that his military operations and aspirations should be directed against Dacia so as to stabilize the Danube frontier, and then, less than a decade later, against Parthia in the east, a campaign from which he did not return.

Yet it seems unlikely that a mere senator, and one not greatly experienced in matters military, would undertake to offer advice to the masterful general. Nor does it appear probable that the monograph was a preliminary effort to gather together material about Germany which was to be used in such graphic detail and vividness in the large works which were to follow. For whatever reason, Tacitus was evidently intrigued by this "noble" people to such a degree that he decided to pass on the results of his researches to the educated aristocracy of Rome.

There is no evidence that Tacitus ever saw Germany himself, but it is not unlikely. His prime literary source was Pliny the Elder's history of the wars in Germany, in which the latter had taken part; this was supplemented by information obtained from merchants and travelers who had visited the North. The writing of the ethnography of a country or people had a lengthy tradition, and Tacitus tried his hand at it in this work.

The *Dialogue on Orators* is the third and most controversial of Tacitus' works. Tacitus' name is absent from it in manuscript, and its style differs from that of the other works so greatly that Tacitean authorship has been totally denied or, if granted, a date of approximately 80 has been proposed for it, when Tacitus would have been about twenty-five years old. The *Dialogue* is based on Ciceronian antecedents and is Ciceronian in style and vocabulary; sentences are long and periodic rather than short, brusque, and lapidary. The difference has been explained away by suggesting that Tacitus wrote the work in his youth and then, in the years of silence under Domitian, developed the style that was peculiarly his own. Not that the champions of non-Tacitean authorship were content even with this. The work which we have, they argued, was by Titinius Capito, or was the *De causis corruptae eloquentiae* ("On the causes of the decline of oratorical eloquence") of the great master of rhetoric, Quintilian himself. These views have in recent years generally lost favor; perhaps the greatest change in Tacitean studies of the last generation is the acceptance of the work as genuinely Tacitus' and the down-dating of it by some thirty years. Today, it is safe to say, *pace* a few diehards, some of whom now favor the years 95–97, that Tacitus wrote this strange work in the first decade of the second century A.D. It is dedicated to Fabius Justus, consul in 102; the presentation of a literary piece to a friend upon the occasion of a significant event in his life was a not uncommon practice in ancient times. That year may not be the precise one of composition; the range 102–107 may well be safer. But the exact date is less important than the general period. How can one explain the style, and the occasion?

It has already been mentioned that Tacitus played a key role in the prosecution of Marius Priscus in 100. His address, Pliny had said, had been marked with majesty (he had spoken σεμνῶς), and in the year 97, upon the occasion of Verginius Rufus' death, Tacitus delivered the funeral address most eloquently (Pliny calls him *laudator eloquentissimus*). In September 100, Pliny delivered his long praise of the emperor Trajan. Tacitus may well have determined, during that year, to withdraw from oratory to devote himself to a higher study, history—convinced that the great days of oratory were gone and that its chief purpose now was for display. Similarly, in the *Dialogue*, Maternus decides to retire from the law courts to spend his time on a higher pursuit, poetry. The relationship between poetry and history in antiquity was very close; Quintilian speaks of history as a kind of poetry without the exigencies of metrical form (10.1.31). Maternus, no doubt, represents the author in the discussion; the reasons given in his closing speech for the decline of oratory go well with Tacitus' views expressed throughout the other works. Pliny, puffed up with his great triumph of language and endurance, must have felt a little deflated when his friend and hero decided that oratory was a field no longer worthy of his talents. The *Dialogue*, then, might very well be Tacitus' swan song to oratory.

But why is the style so different from all else by Tacitus? The ability and capacity to write in various styles, almost, as it were, to change clothes, were the marks of the trained rhetorician, who realized that different genres of literature required different garbs. In a genre in which Cicero was the acknowledged master, nothing was more appropriate than the Ciceronian garb. Individuals can write different works in different styles at the same time; certainly one should no longer attempt to base a date for the *Dialogue* on its stylistic uniqueness in the corpus of Tacitus' works.

When Tacitus published the *Dialogue,* he was already at work on the *Histories,* which covered the years 69–96. He must have spent much of this decade on the *Histories,* and then he turned to the *Annals,* in which he went back to the death of Augustus and wrote the history of Tiberius, Gaius (better known as Caligula), Claudius, and Nero, in other words, the years 14–68.

These two works comprised thirty books, a figure recorded by Saint Jerome. How they were divided is a matter of controversy. Tradition assigns fourteen to the *Histories,* sixteen to the *Annals,* but there are those who argue for a hexadic grouping of books. The *Histories* will then have contained twelve, six on Vespasian, six on Titus and Domitian, and the *Annals* eighteen, six on Tiberius, six on Gaius and Claudius, and six on Nero.

The *Histories* and the *Annals* are sufficient to guarantee Tacitus' place among the great historians of all time, for they are his most significant and most probing examinations of the behavior of men and states. But further discussion of them is beyond the scope of this introductory essay. The three shorter works with which this volume deals, frequently dubbed the *opera minora,* "lesser works," represent an important phase of Tacitus' development as an historian. They are not merely individual pamphlets; rather they show the development of the insight and the germs of the basic pessimism which mark the longer works. A German translation of the trio was entitled *Die historischen Versuche,* "The Historical Attempts" (Karl Büchner, *Publius Cornelius Tacitus, Agricola, Germania, Dialogus de Oratoribus: Die historischen Versuche,* 3rd ed. by Reinhard Häussler [Stuttgart, 1985]). It is a good title, for there is much of the stuff of history in them.

Consequently, consideration of these works must take into account what is perhaps the basic question upon which hangs judgment regarding Tacitus' stature as an historian. There are already evident here hints of his dissatisfaction with the principate as a form of government, the viewpoint that is so starkly presented in the *Annals.* Is it thus fair to say that Tacitus always was intellectually opposed to the imperial regime and yearned for the "glorious" days of the republic? Is not then his claim, put forth at the beginning of the *Annals*, that he will write *sine ira et studio*, "without prejudice and without favor," a sham?

It is my view that the answer to both questions must be negative. In spite of the insistence of several distinguished scholars that Tacitus' political outlook never changed in its essence and was always dark and pessimistic, it appears to me that there is a gradual deepening of his emotions from work to work. His welcome of the reigns of Nerva and Trajan, the former of whom had reconciled the rule of a *princeps* and the individual freedom of his subjects, was sincere and deeply felt. At this stage of his historical work, he was prepared to inveigh against one emperor or another, but not against the empire. The contrast between the new order and the reign of Domitian was too great not to have been appreciated. But it was one of the anomalies of the Roman empire that autocracy tended to make its greatest strides precisely under those men who were considered the good emperors, because they were so respected and so capable that more and more of the functions of government, including many properly in the senate's sphere, passed almost imperceptibly into their hands. As the years of Trajan's reign passed one after the other and Tacitus realized that the senate, the symbol of republican government, though given its external meed of honor, had become in actuality an anachronism, his mood darkened. In the *Annals* he is, among other things, concerned with the baneful effects of the principate's powers upon the character of the rulers and writes of the gradual disintegration of Tiberius with the bitter memories of Domitian foremost in his mind. Yet he is not being intentionally fraudulent; there is no instance of factual error in his works that can be ascribed to ulterior motives. It is in Tacitus' probing of the depths of the human mind that his interpretation of the motives of the individual is colored by his remembrance of things past. It is here that his powers of suggestion, his skill in innuendo, weigh so heavily; he is masterful in presenting evidence on both sides of a question so that the view that he wishes remembered will be presented last and at greater length than the opposing one; the view favored is invariably the one that will do the greatest harm to the individual involved.

Is Tacitus therefore to be denied the title of "historian"? In a scientific age, it is a commonplace that history should, and must, be "objective." But, it may perhaps reasonably be asked, has there ever been an "objective" historian? We must insist upon scrupulous treatment of facts, but facts must always be interpreted, judgments must be made, suggestions concerning motives must be advanced, and these interpretations, judgments, and suggestions are made by human beings who are molded by their own experiences. History is not written in a vacuum, nor by machines; it is written by fallible individuals, no two of whom will likely agree on every facet of a series of events. In our own days, we need recall no more than the varying judgments of Adolf Hitler that have issued forth in England and the United States; if one assumes that all students of Hitler have the same basic stock of material upon which to draw, one often wonders how judgments so disparate can be drawn from them.

So it was with Tacitus. A child of his age, as are all human beings to a greater or lesser degree, his outlook was conditioned by his personal experience, and, as he grew older, he began to realize that the reconciliation which he had hailed in 98 was an actual impossibility. For he became aware of the fundamental problem of the principate, which is that of deceit. Beginning with Augustus' first settlement after the battle of Actium in 31 B.C., effective control of the empire was in the hands of the emperor, who was commander-in-chief of the armies and had tremendous financial resources at his disposal, as well as the unique prestige that his position helped bestow upon him. The *respublica restituta,* the restored republic of which Augustus boasted in the record of his achievements that he composed late in life, the *Res Gestae,* could not actually exist, for the seat of effective power had shifted from the senate to the emperor. Yet, for the sake of appearance and the morale of the senatorial order, it must seem to exist; this could not be accomplished without deception and fraud. Whether the new form of government was good or bad, whether Augustus himself was an idealistic ruler or a self-seeking power politician are questions that need not be discussed here. But it is certain that they are questions that Tacitus considered in the maturity of years, and the *Annals* give us his answers. And it is likewise certain that his penetrating insight into the interrelationships of men and events has rarely, if ever, been surpassed; generations that have witnessed great heights of power politics and the reigns of vicious tyrants can still find many pertinent judgments in Tacitus' pages. It used to be said that Tacitus painted individuals worse than they could possibly be; the twentieth century has learned to know how ruthless and morally degraded human beings can become under pressure.

THE PRINCIPATE

The first century B.C. witnessed the constant struggle for the first position in the state among several of Rome's greatest figures,

first Marius and Sulla, then Pompey, Crassus, and Caesar, and
ultimately, after Caesar's assassination on the Ides of March, 44,
between Antony and Octavian, Caesar's adopted grandnephew.
When the young Caesar, as Octavian was officially known, was
victorious over Antony and the Egyptian queen Cleopatra in the
year 31 and then undertook to reestablish the republican consti-
tution, as far as it seemed feasible to do so, he resigned the state
to the jurisdiction of the senate and the Roman people in Janu-
ary, 27. In gratitude, the senate honored him with the name Augustus and regularized his unique position in the state by the
grant of specified powers.

We need not mention all these. Suffice it to say that Augustus
was thereafter known as the *princeps*, the "First Citizen," from
which word our term "the principate" derives. The keys to his
power in the state were his control over most of the revenues
and the military might of the empire and, on a personal basis,
his overriding *auctoritas*, which means "prestige" or "influence"
rather than "authority." It was a personal quality that indicated
that the individual had the respect of others, who looked to him
for leadership and policy. Augustus was able to claim that he
had restored the republic because none of his own powers was
without precedent or considered "unconstitutional." The other
organs of the state continued to exist and function: the senate
and the magistrates were regularized after the confusions of
the civil wars, and the equestrians, the wealthy business class,
gained in importance.

The senate, whose membership had reached about one thousand under Caesar, was reduced to the traditional number of six
hundred. Although very little real power remained in the senate's control, it continued as the state's social aristocracy, passed
legislation, and designated the governors of numerous provinces, essentially those without military garrisons. Entry to the
senate came with election to the most junior of the offices that
continued to compose the *cursus honorum*, the "career of public
offices."

The quaestorship remained the lowest magistracy that brought
with it lifetime membership in the senate. The duties of the
quaestors were financial. The aediles, the next-higher officials,
were largely concerned with the proper functioning of the city
of Rome. The praetors dealt with judicial matters, while the consulship, as in the republic, conferred "nobility" upon those who
held it and made them eligible for the governorship of the most
important provinces, both those under the emperor's jurisdiction and those under the senate's.

Without the availability of senators the emperor could not have governed the vast extent of the empire. But he also called upon the talents of the equestrian order to govern smaller provinces, to handle financial matters, and to hold some of the most crucial positions in the bureaucracy, such as the prefecture of Egypt, the prefecture of the praetorian guard, the imperial bodyguard, and the prefecture of the *vigiles,* who fulfilled the duties of police and fire protection in the city of Rome. The emperor also made use of freedmen, one-time slaves, and slaves in his own household. Freedmen often rose to heights of enormous power and influence, particularly under the emperor Claudius.

Various priesthoods also conferred distinction and influence. Augustus became the chief priest of the state, the *pontifex maximus,* long after his power had become secure, because he did not wish to depose the incumbent. From 12 B.C. on, the emperor always automatically became *pontifex maximus.* The colleges of the *pontifices* and the *augures* retained their primacy and distinction; the other two of the major priesthoods were the *quindecimviri sacris faciundis* and the *septemviri epulonum.* The former were a body of fifteen charged with responsibility for state festivals, the latter a body of seven responsible for public banquets.

The public bureaucracy of the early principate was very small. Without the assistance of several thousand men from the groups mentioned above, the emperor would have been unable to govern. With their assistance and cooperation, provinces had their governors, legions their commanders, revenues were collected, petitions heard and answered. The emperor's powers were essentially limitless, if he desired them to be, but an emperor's reputation depended, above all, on his relations with the senate and the upper orders of society. Domitian "waged war" on the senate, Trajan cultivated it. Consequently, Domitian was assassinated and his memory condemned, Trajan was styled *optimus princeps.* But in policy and government the two were very much alike.

THE ARMY

Augustus had planned an army of twenty-eight legions. The loss of three in the year A.D. 9 against the German chieftain Arminius reduced that number to twenty-five. At full strength, each legion had about six thousand men. The soldiers were Roman citizens and served for twenty years.

In addition, there were auxiliary forces made up of noncitizens, of whom the total number was approximately equal to that of the legionaries. These men made up the major part of the cavalry forces and offered specialities that Italians lacked, for example, as slingers and archers. The auxiliaries served for twenty-five years and received citizenship upon discharge.

Britain was conquered by four legions, II Augusta, IX Hispana, XIV Gemina Martia, and XX Valeria Victrix. Three of these were still in Britain when Agricola arrived as governor, with the fourteenth replaced by II Adiutrix. Each was housed in a fort: II Augusta, at Caerleon in southern Wales; II Adiutrix, at Chester facing northern Wales; XX, at Wroxeter a bit farther south; and IX, at York, opposite the great tribe of the Brigantes. With auxiliaries, Agricola commanded a total force of some 40,000 to 45,000 men.

At the time when Tacitus composed the *Germania*, eight legions were stationed along the Rhine frontier in the provinces of Upper and Lower Germany. Trajan reduced them to four, two in each province.

Selected Bibliography

GENERAL

Benario, H. W. *An Introduction to Tacitus*. Athens, Ga.: University of Georgia Press, 1975.
The Cambridge Ancient History. Vol. 10, *The Augustan Empire, 44 B.C.–A.D. 70*; and vol. 11, *The Imperial Peace, A.D. 70–192*. Cambridge: Cambridge University Press, 1934 and 1936.
Dudley, D. R. *The World of Tacitus*. Boston: Little, Brown, 1968.
Fritz, K. von. "Tacitus, Agricola, Domitian, and the Problem of the Principate." *Classical Philology* 52 (1957): 73–97.
Goodyear, F. R. D. *Tacitus*. Greece & Rome, New Surveys in the Classics, no. 4. Oxford: Clarendon Press, 1970.
Goodyear, F. R. D. "Tacitus." In *Cambridge History of Classical Literature* 2:642–55. Cambridge: Cambridge University Press, 1982.
Leeman, A. D. *Orationis Ratio: The Stylistic Theories and Practice of the Roman Orators, Historians and Philosophers*. Pp. 320–23, 337–60. Amsterdam: Hakkert, 1963.
Luce, T. J. "Tacitus." In *Ancient Writers: Greece and Rome* 2:1003–33. New York: Scribner, 1982.
Martin, R. *Tacitus*. Berkeley and Los Angeles: University of California Press, 1981.
Mendell, C. W. *Tacitus: The Man and His Work*. New Haven: Yale University Press, 1957.
Syme, R. *Tacitus*. Oxford: Clarendon Press, 1958.
General surveys of Tacitus studies by H. W. Benario, covering the years 1954 through 1983, have appeared in *Classical World* 58 (1964–65): 69–83; 63 (1969–70): 253–67; 71 (1977–78): 1–32; 80 (1986–87): 73–147.

THE PRINCIPATE

Garnsey, P., and R. Saller, *The Early Principate: Augustus to Trajan*. Greece & Rome, New Surveys in the Classics, no. 15. Oxford: Clarendon Press, 1982.
Garzetti, A. *From Tiberius to the Antonines: A History of the Roman Empire AD 14–192*. London: Methuen and Co., 1974.
Hammond, M. *The Antonine Monarchy*. Rome: American Academy in Rome, 1959.
Talbert, R. J. A. *The Senate of Imperial Rome*. Princeton: Princeton University Press, 1984.

THE ARMY

Watson, G. R. *The Roman Soldier.* Ithaca, N.Y.: Cornell University Press, 1969.
Webster, G. *The Roman Imperial Army of the First and Second Centuries A.D.* (3d ed.). Totowa, N.J.: Barnes and Noble, 1985.

AGRICOLA

Birley, A. R. *The Fasti of Roman Britain.* Oxford: Clarendon Press, 1981.
Birley, E. "Britain under the Flavians: Agricola and his Predecessors." In *Roman Britain and the Roman Army,* pp. 10–19. Kendal: T. Wilson, 1953.
Burn, A. R. *Agricola and Roman Britain.* New York: Collier Books, 1962.
Liebeschuetz, W. "The Theme of Liberty in the *Agricola* of Tacitus." *Classical Quarterly* 16 (1966): 126–39.
Richmond, I. A. "Cn. Iulius Agricola." *Journal of Roman Studies* 34 (1944): 34–45.
Stuart, D. R. *Epochs of Greek and Roman Biography.* Berkeley: University of California Press, 1928.

GERMANY

Beare, W. "Tacitus on the Germans." *Greece & Rome* 11 (1964): 64–76.
Benario, H. W. "Tacitus' *Germania* and Modern Germany." *Illinois Classical Studies* 15 (1990) 1:163–75.
Thompson, E. A. *The Early Germans.* Oxford: Oxford University Press, 1965.

DIALOGUE ON ORATORS

Costa, C. D. N. "The 'Dialogus'." In T. A. Dorey, ed., *Tacitus,* pp. 19–34. London: Routledge and Kegan Paul, 1969.
Kennedy, G. *The Art of Rhetoric in the Roman World 300 B.C.–A.D. 300.* Princeton: Princeton University Press, 1972. Pp. 515–23.

The Roman Emperors and Their Reigns from Augustus to Hadrian

Augustus	B.C. 27–A.D.	14
Tiberius		14–37
Gaius (Caligula)		37–41
Claudius		41–54
Nero		54–68
Galba		68–69
Otho		69
Vitellius		69
Vespasian		69–79
Titus		79–81
Domitian		81–96
Nerva		96–98
Trajan		98–117
Hadrian		117–138

Agricola

Gnaeus Julius Agricola was born in A.D. 40. His political career is marked by a steady advance through the *cursus honorum*, culminating in the consulship at an age some five years before the "normal" or "customary" year, although it is difficult to speak of a norm during the principate when a man could advance by as many as ten years depending upon the prestige of his family and the number of children whom he sired, since each child brought remission of one year from the minimum age. Agricola's first public duties were in Britain as military tribune in 60, followed by the quaestorship in 64, when he served in Asia, the tribunate of the plebs in 66, and the praetorship in 68. That year saw the beginning of the upheaval of civil war, and before long he cast his lot with the party of Vespasian, a wise choice, as later events proved. In 70 he was returned to Britain as commander of *legio XX Valeria Victrix,* and followed this tour of duty with the governorship of Aquitania as *legatus Augusti pro praetore*, with praetorian rank, from 74 to 76. He was recalled to Rome to undertake the highest post of the regular *cursus* as suffect consul in 77. In that year, he married his daughter to Tacitus and received the high honor of a major priesthood, being appointed a *pontifex.* He then (for the date, see the discussion below) went for the third time to Britain, this time as *legatus Augusti pro praetore,* with consular rank, where for seven years as governor he accomplished some of Rome's most spectacular military achievements. After his recall by Domitian, whether for reasons of military and political expediency or because of jealousy, he held no further public office, passing up the governorship of Asia, which he could rightly have considered his due in the year 90. He died three years later, aged 53, a figure of some import in his own day, who nonetheless looms much larger for us than any other public servant during the long span of the principate, save for the emperors; for his son-in-law's hope that the reputation of his wife's father would survive the passage of time was fulfilled. Tacitus' tribute to Agricola was the gift of immortality.

The only chronological problem in Agricola's life concerns the date of his departure for Britain after his consulship and when,

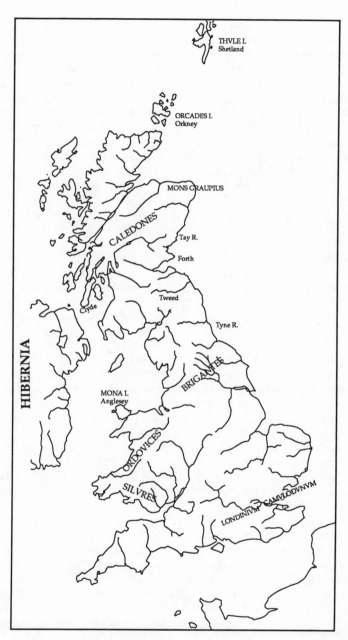

Britain in Roman times

correspondingly, the seventh, last, and decisive year of his tenure came. The choices are between the periods 77–83 and 78–84; the only precise clues are those furnished by Tacitus himself, who at the end of chapter 9 says that Agricola, after his consulship, was immediately (*statim*) appointed governor of Britain and at the beginning of chapter eighteen remarks that Agricola arrived in midsummer (*media iam aestate*) when the troops thought it was too late for a campaigning season. Other arguments are based upon the relationship of events in Britain with those of Germany, particularly the arrival of the Usipi in Britain (chapter 28). My conviction, although I herein disagree with the majority of modern scholars, is that the Latin text, when read without predilections, practically demands a close temporal relationship among consulship, celebration of the marriage, appointment as governor, and arrival in Britain, with the result that I choose the years 77–83 for Agricola's governorship.

Tacitus' monograph is easily divided into sections, wherein biography and history are presented in alternate layers as well as being interwoven even in the most obviously biographical parts. He begins with a prooemium, covering three chapters. Agricola's birth, early life and training, and his political career up to his governorship of Britain occupy chapters 4 through 9. The next three are concerned with the geography of the island and ethnography of its peoples, and chapters 13 through 17 survey the past history of Rome's relations with Britain and the achievements of Agricola's predecessors. The main and central part of the work covers approximately half its entire length; it details the campaigns and administrative achievements of Agricola in chapters 18 through 38, and is highlighted by the powerful speeches of Calgacus and Agricola in chapters 30 through 34. Chapters 39 through 43 relate his recall and the last years of his life. An epilogue of three chapters (44 through 46) balances the prooemium, culminating in a magnificent, though rhetorical, intimation of immortality.

Biography was a form of literature very congenial to the Romans, with a long tradition from the days of the republic. Since the Romans believed that judgment of a man's life depended upon his actions, the custom of delivering laudatory addresses at his funeral, *laudationes*, gave him a bit of immortality, as did the bust in the atrium of the family house with the attached *elogium*, an inscription which recorded the most important offices that the deceased had held and his most significant achievements.

Tomb monuments and public buildings which bore the individual's name kept his reputation, and that of his family, in the public eye. So too did the written exposition of his life, which enabled a much wider audience to become more closely acquainted with the great man's life, which could be used as an exemplar for others. Biography thus tended to be both a eulogy and an historical document; the value of the latter depended greatly upon the abilities of the writer and the availability of information about the subject.

The best-known biography in Latin is that of Suetonius. The purpose was to describe an individual rather than produce an historical document. Consequently, chronology is largely ignored, and similar material is grouped together. Tacitus approached his task differently. He was writing about a man whom he had known very well and with whom he had often spoken. Agricola had been responsible for an enormous increase in knowledge about the island of Britain, with which Tacitus was able to correct and expand earlier belief. Agricola had accomplished extraordinary deeds in government and warfare, which Tacitus wished to relate within the larger context of Rome's relationship with the island and its people. He therefore made the focus of his biography Agricola's seven years of command in the province. History is well served, but all others are given very brief treatment. The hero of the work could not have any significant rivals.

Tacitus gives relatively few details about the geography of the land and the various battles and campaigns. To a Roman reader who knew little about Britain, where very few communities or topographical details could be identified, precision was unimportant, and impossible. It was the grand sweep of events, the ebb and flow, which counted, as did the varying delineations of viewpoint presented in the paired speeches of the barbarian chieftain and the Roman governor in chapters 30 to 34. Yet Tacitus' reports of the land are remarkably accurate, as archaeology has confirmed. Not only do we know a great deal about Agricola, we know a great deal about what he did, and where, and under what circumstances.

Agricola

Chapters 1–3. Introduction to the entire work and discussion of the tradition of biography.

1. *Biography at Rome has a long and honorable tradition, but the present times are hostile to the biographies of good men.*

The practice of recording for posterity the deeds and characters of famous men, which was common in times past, has not even in our own times been ignored by an age disdainful of its own history, whenever some great and outstanding excellence has overcome and risen above a fault common to states both great and small, that is, not to understand and yet to hate that which is right. But, just as it was easy and there was greater opportunity among our ancestors to do deeds worthy of record, so everyone who was most renowned for talent was motivated only by the reward of a good conscience to transmit the record of excellence without partiality or desire of personal gain. Many even considered it confidence in their characters rather than arrogance to relate their own lives, nor was that an indication of lack of integrity or a source of reproach for Rutilius[1] or Scaurus.[2] So greatly are examples of excellence most highly cherished in the very periods in which they are most easily produced. But now I have had to ask for pardon as I undertake to relate the life of a deceased man, pardon which I would not have sought had I intended to bring charges against him. So cruel and hostile to excellence are the times.

2. *Under Domitian books were burned as the emperor strove to crush all intellectual opposition. Freedom of speech disappeared.*

We read that it was a capital crime when Thrasea Paetus and Helvidius Priscus were praised by Arulenus Rusticus and Heren-

---

[1] P. Rutilius Rufus, consul in 105 B.C., was legate in the province of Asia in 95. An upright and virtuous man, he was accused of extortion by the tax collectors, against whose claims he protected the provincials, and, upon conviction, went into exile among the very provincials he had been accused of plundering.

[2] M. Aemilius Scaurus, consul in 115 and 107 B.C. and censor in 109, was for long *princeps senatus*.

nius Senecio, respectively,[3] and that violence was directed not only against the authors themselves but also against their books, with the assignment given to the commission of three men[4] to burn in the comitium and the forum[5] the achievements of the most celebrated talents. Surely they thought that the voice of the Roman people and the independence of the senate and the conscience of the human race were destroyed by that fire; and, in addition, they expelled the philosophers and drove all intellectual activity into exile, so that nothing honorable might anywhere meet one's gaze. We certainly displayed extraordinary submission, and just as a former age witnessed the extreme of liberty, so did we the extreme of slavery, when even the opportunity to speak and listen was wrested from us by espionage. We would also have lost our very memories, together with freedom of speech, if it were equally in our power to forget as to be silent.

3. *With Nerva and Trajan a new age has begun, where people can say what they wish. Talent recovers slowly; nonetheless, Tacitus tries his hand with this tribute to his father-in-law.*

Now at last our spirit returns; but, although the emperor Nerva, at the very beginning of a most happy age, united two things formerly incompatible, the rule of one man and personal freedom, and although the emperor Trajan daily increases the good fortune of the times, and although the well-being of the people has not only expressed hope and a prayer for the future but also has received the fulfillment and realization of the prayer itself, yet by the nature of human weakness remedies are slower to take effect than their ills. And as our bodies grow slowly and are quickly destroyed, so too could one more readily crush genius and its activities than bring them back; for a certain pleasure in doing nothing comes over one, and the slothfulness that is hated at first is at the last esteemed. What if, for a period of fifteen years, a great span of human life, many men perished by natural deaths, and all the most capable because of the emperor's cruelty? We few indeed have outlived not only others but also, if I

---

[3]Paetus, the leader of the Stoic opposition against Nero, and Helvidius, his son-in-law, were put to death by Nero and Vespasian, respectively. See Tacitus, *Annals* XVI. 21ff., and Suetonius, *Vespasian* XV.

[4]The *triumviri capitales* were minor magistrates responsible for the execution of those condemned on capital charges. Book burning was normally assigned to their superiors, the aediles.

[5]The comitium was an open area in the northwestern part of the forum, adjacent to the senate-house.

may use the expression, ourselves, with so many years plucked from the middle of our lives, years in which those of us who were young reached maturity, and the mature approached the very limits of extreme old age, in silence. Nonetheless, it will not be a source of regret to have written down the recollection of our former servitude and the record of our present good, even with a style unskilled and crude. This book, in the meantime, intended to honor my father-in-law, Agricola, will be praised for or excused by its expression of filial devotion.

Chapters 4–9. Agricola's origin, education, and career up to the governorship of Britain.

4. *Born in Gallia Narbonensis into a senatorial family, Agricola was too enraptured of philosophy for one of his class. But good sense won out.*

Gnaeus Julius Agricola was born in the ancient and famous city of Forum Julii.[6] Both his grandfathers held the office of procurator of the emperor and thereby attained the nobility of the equestrian order. His father, Julius Graecinus, was a senator, renowned for his dedication to oratory and philosophy, and by these very qualities he earned the hatred of the emperor Gaius, for, when ordered to prosecute Marcus Silanus, he refused and was then put to death.[7] His mother was Julia Procilla, a woman of remarkable purity of character. Raised by her with care and affection, he passed his childhood and teens by devoting himself to all liberal pursuits. He was protected from enticements of wrongdoers not only by his own good and upright character, but also by the fact that, from early childhood, he lived in Marseilles and studied there. Marseilles was characterized by a well-balanced mixture of Greek sophistication and the frugality that is typical of a province of the empire. I remember that he used to say that, early in his life, he would have devoted himself too enthusiastically to the study of philosophy, to an extent greater than was fitting for a Roman who was also a member of the senatorial class, had not the wisdom of his mother restrained his eager and excited spirit. Certainly his lofty and talented nature yearned for the beautiful ideal of great and noble glory with greater passion than caution. Soon the discernment of age calmed him down, yet he retained from his contact with philosophy a sense of proportion that is very difficult to acquire.

[6] The modern Fréjus on the French Riviera.
[7] The year was A.D. 40; Silanus died early in 38, so there was no immediate relationship between Graecinus' refusal and his death.

5. *Having begun military service in Britain when the province was almost destroyed by the revolt of Boudicca, Agricola devoted himself to
duty and became a respected officer.*

His first military service was in Britain under Suetonius Paulinus, a conscientious and cautious general, when he had been
chosen to be the latter's aide; his performance satisfied his commander. Agricola did not behave with the license of young men
who turn their military service into dissipation, nor did he, displaying no energy, take advantage of his rank of tribune and his
inexperience to pursue his personal pleasure and obtain leaves
of absence. Rather he spent his time getting to know the province, becoming known to the army, learning from experienced
men, taking the best men as models, seeking nothing for personal advantage, refusing no assignment because of fear, and
performing his duties, simultaneously cautious and energetic.
Nor was Britain ever more in turmoil and its possession more in
doubt: discharged veterans had been butchered, colonies set
afire, armies destroyed. At that time the struggle was for survival, soon it was to be for conquest. Although all these things
were accomplished by the strategy and generalship of someone
else and the overall control and the glory of the recovery of the
province fell to the commander, yet the young Agricola gained
skill and experience and incentive, and the desire for military
glory came to his mind, a desire that is dangerous in times when
outstanding men are suspect and there is as much peril from a
great reputation as from a bad one.

6. *Over the next half-dozen years, Agricola married and served as
quaestor in Asia and praetor in Rome, with integrity and caution. After
the death of Nero, he was appointed by the emperor Galba to investigate
misappropriations of temple treasures.*

When he had returned from Britain to Rome to stand for public
office, he married Domitia Decidiana, a lady of eminent ancestry. That marriage proved a source of honor and support for him
as he strove for advancement. They lived together in wondrous
harmony, with mutual affection and particular regard for each
other, a trait that deserves greater praise in a good wife as it mer-
its greater reproach in a bad one. When the quaestors drew lots,
Agricola was assigned to the province of Asia under the governorship of Salvius Titianus.[8] Neither the place nor the man cor-

[8]Brother of the future emperor Otho, Agricola served under him only for part
of his term as quaestor.

rupted Agricola, although the province was wealthy and wide open to wrongdoers, and the governor, who enriched himself in every manner, was willing to secure mutual concealment of crime by the most extreme leniency. His family was increased there by a daughter, who was both support for his public career and consolation, for he soon lost an older son. Then he passed the time between his quaestorship and his tribunate of the people in inactivity and leisure, and he did not act differently even while he was tribune, since he knew that, in the reign of Nero, idleness was considered wisdom. His praetorship was similar in terms of its peaceful inactivity, for he had not been assigned to preside over a court. He presented public games and other trivialities of his office with a nice mixture of restraint and extravagance, with the result that his reputation increased all the more as he avoided excess. Then, when he had been appointed by the emperor Galba to conduct an investigation of temple holdings, he carried this out with the greatest of integrity, so that the state seemed to have suffered the sacrilege of no one other than Nero.

7. *In the year 69, his mother was murdered and he himself went over to the side of Vespasian. He was appointed commander of the Twentieth Legion in Britain.*

The next year inflicted a terrible wound on his spirit and home. For the fleet of Otho, cruising like brigands, while it plundered Intimilium (it is located in Liguria)[9] as if it were an enemy city, murdered Agricola's mother on her estate, ravaged the estate, and carried off much of the wealth left by his father. This wealth was the cause of her murder. Then, when Agricola had left Rome to perform the rites of a dutiful son in honor of his mother, the news came to him en route that Vespasian had laid claim to the empire, and he immediately gave the latter his support. Mucianus controlled the government and Rome before Vespasian arrived in the capital, since Domitian was still a young man[10] and took advantage of his father's high state only to have a riotous time. After Agricola had been assigned to enroll troops and had done it with integrity and vigor, Mucianus put him in command of the Twentieth Legion,[11] which had reluctantly sworn allegiance to Vespasian and where his predecessor was said to be acting treacherously. The legion was undisciplined and terrifying even to consular legates, and the present com-

[9] The modern Ventimiglia on the Italian Riviera.
[10] He was then eighteen years old.
[11] The twentieth legion was one of four in Britain.

mander, only of praetorian rank, was powerless to control it, whether because of his nature or that of his soldiers. Thus Agricola, chosen both to succeed and to punish, preferred, with the most unusual modesty, to seem to have found good men rather than to have made them good.

8. *When Petilius Cerialis became governor, Agricola had opportunities for independent action and personal success. But he never forgot his subordinate position.*

Vettius Bolanus then governed Britain, with a more peaceful manner than was appropriate for a warlike province. Agricola controlled his energy and restrained his enthusiasm in order not to rise above his position, since he was practiced in obedience and trained to join the advantageous with the honorable. Then, in a short time, Britain received Petilius Cerialis, a man of consular rank, as its governor. Agricola's talents had an opportunity to assert themselves. At first Cerialis shared with him only toils and dangers, but soon also glory: he often put him in command of part of the army to test him, sometimes, as a result of his success, in command of larger forces. Nor did Agricola ever boast of his achievements to enhance his own reputation: he referred his good fortune to the general as the man responsible, since he was a junior officer. Thus, by his conscientious devotion to duty and his modesty in speech, he escaped envy but was not without glory.

9. *Upon his return to Rome, Agricola was made a patrician and appointed governor of the province of Aquitania. After fewer than three years there, he was appointed consul, made a pontifex, and designated governor of Britain.*

Upon his return from his position as commander of the legion, the deified Vespasian enrolled him among the patricians and then appointed him governor of the province of Aquitania, a post of particularly great prestige because of the responsibility of its administration and one that brought expectation of a consulship, for which the emperor had marked him out. There are quite a few who believe that the characters of soldiers lack sophistication, on the grounds that the procedure of military justice, being unopposed and rather heavy-handed and accomplishing most things summarily, does not give opportunity for the skill of the forum. Yet Agricola, with his innate good sense, acted with ease and justice although among civilians. Now, indeed, the periods of business and relaxation were separated:

whenever circuit courts demanded his attention, he was serious, attentive, stern, and yet more often compassionate: when he had done his duty, he put aside the appearance of power; he had avoided gloominess, arrogance, and avarice.[12] Nor in his case, and this is a rare occurrence, did his easy-going manner lessen his prestige or his sternness lessen affection. It would be an insult to his good qualities to speak of integrity and self-restraint in so great a man. He did not even seek renown, for which even good men often have a yearning, by ostentatious display of excellence or by chicanery: with no desire for rivalry with his fellow governors nor dispute with procurators,[13] he considered it discreditable to be superior to them and disgraceful to be worsted. He was kept in that position for less than three years and was recalled with immediate hope of the consulship; the report that Britain was being assigned him as his province accompanied him, not because of any statements of his on this matter, but because it seemed right. Rumor is by no means always wrong; sometimes it even chooses the person. During his consulship, he betrothed his daughter, at that time a girl of outstanding promise, to me, a young man, and after his consulship gave her to me in marriage; he was at once put in command of Britain and was also appointed a pontifex.

Chapters 10–12. Geography and ethnography of Britain.

10. *Britain's location and shape. The sea is sluggish and flows deeply into the land.*

I shall relate the geography and ethnology of Britain, which have been recorded by many authors, not to produce a comparison of literary skill or talent, but because it was then for the first time completely conquered. Thus material that my predecessors embellished with rhetorical skill because it had not yet been ascertained will be presented with confidence in the facts. Britain, which is the largest island of which the Romans know, in its geographical extent and situation reaches toward Germany on the east and toward Spain on the west, and is even within view of the Gauls on the south; its north, with no lands facing it, is beaten by a vast open sea. Livy, the most polished writer of the old days, and Fabius Rusticus, the most polished of recent times, have likened the shape of the whole of Britain to an

---

[12] This last clause destroys the continuity of Tacitus' development. It should perhaps be rejected as a marginal gloss which was inserted into the text.
[13] The procurators were the imperial financial officers.

oblong dish or a double-edged axe. And that is its appearance south of Caledonia, from which the description spread to the whole. But, for those who have gone on, the vast and huge extent of land, extending from what is the farthest shore, is narrowed into the shape of a wedge, so to speak. A Roman fleet then for the first time sailed around this shore of the most distant sea and confirmed that Britain was an island, and at the same time discovered and subdued islands that had been unknown up to this time, which men call the Orcades.[14] And Thule was only seen from far off, since their orders went only so far and winter was approaching. But the report is that the sea, sluggish and heavy to rowers, is not even raised by the winds like others (I believe because lands and mountains, the source and opportunity for storms, are less common) and the heavy mass of the never-ending sea is more slowly stirred. It is not within the sphere of this work to investigate the nature and tides of the ocean, and many have reported them: I would add one thing, that nowhere does the sea hold sway more widely and it directs many currents hither and thither, nor does it ebb and flow only as far as the coastline, but it flows deep inland and winds around there, and is found even among ridges and mountains as though in its own domain.

11. *Britain was originally occupied by the Gauls.*

But it is insufficiently known, as is common when dealing with barbarians, whether the first inhabitants of Britain were native-born or immigrants. Their physical characteristics are varied, and there are arguments based on this variation. For the red hair and huge limbs of the inhabitants of Caledonia are an indication of German origin; the swarthy complexions and generally curly hair of the Silures, and their location facing Spain, give credence to the belief that Iberians of old crossed over and occupied these places; those nearest the Gauls are also like them, whether because the influence of their origin endures or because, since the lands tend in opposite directions,[15] the same climate gave their bodies the same appearance. Nevertheless, it seems feasible, to one considering the question as a whole, that the Gauls occupied the neighboring island. You would find in Britain their religious rites and their beliefs in superstitions; their language is

---

[14]The Orkney Islands.

[15]An awkward way of saying that Gaul looks to the north and Britain to the south.

not very different, there is the same boldness in demanding dangers and the same dread in fleeing them when they have come. Nonetheless, the Britons display more bravery, since they are a people whom extended peace has not yet weakened. For we have heard that the Gauls too were renowned in wars; soon slothfulness came in together with peace, after manliness and liberty alike were lost. This happened in time past to those of the Britons who had been conquered; the rest remain as the Gauls used to be.

12. *The Britons' method of fighting, the climate, crops, and minerals.*

Their strength is in infantry; certain tribes also fight from a chariot. The charioteer is the more honorable, his retainers fight in his defense. Formerly they obeyed kings, now they are torn by factions and partisan feelings because of chieftains. Nor is anything more advantageous for us in dealing with very strong peoples than the fact that they do not confer for the common good.[16] Rarely do two or three states join together to ward off a common danger: thus they fight one by one and are without exception conquered.

The climate is terrible because of frequent rains and fogs; the bitterness of cold is not present. The days are longer than they are in our world; the night is bright and, in the farthest part of Britain, short, so that one could barely separate evening from dawn. But they claim that the gleam of the sun is seen throughout the night if clouds do not interfere and that the sun does not set or rise but passes through the horizon. Certainly the most distant flat stretches of land, with their low-lying shadow, do not produce darkness high up, and night falls below the sky and stars.

The soil produces crops and is fertile, except for the olive and the vine and other things that customarily grow in warmer lands. The crops mature slowly and grow quickly; the cause of both occurrences is the same, the abundant moisture of the land and climate. Britain possesses gold and silver and other metals; these are the reward of conquest. The ocean also produces pearls, but they are dark and spotted. Certain people think that the pearl-fishers lack skill, for in the Persian Gulf the pearls are torn from the rocks, living and breathing, while in Britain they are collected just as they have been cast up. I should more readily believe that the pearls lack quality than that we lack avarice.

[16]See *Germany* 33.

Chapters 13–17. Stages in Rome's conquest of Britain up to the decade of the 70s.

13. *Julius Caesar first invaded Britain, but the island was ignored by Augustus and Tiberius. Gaius Caesar (Caligula) planned a campaign, but it was Claudius who began the conquest.*

The Britons themselves readily endure the levy and tributes and the duties of subjects that are imposed if abuses are absent: these they hardly tolerate, since they have thus far been sufficiently tamed to obey but not yet to be slaves. The deified Julius, then, who was the first of all the Romans to invade Britain with an army, although he terrified the natives with a successful battle and got possession of the shore, can be said to have pointed Britain out to posterity, not to have handed it over. Soon there were civil wars and the arms of the dynasts were turned against the state, and Britain was long forgotten even in peace: this the deified Augustus called policy; Tiberius, precedent. It is generally agreed that Gaius Caesar had thought about the invasion of Britain, if he had not been quick to regret it because of his changeable nature, and his great enterprises against Germany had not been fruitless. The deified Claudius was the one who renewed the operation, with legions and auxiliaries transported there and Vespasian taken along to share in the campaign, the first step of the fortune that was soon to come: tribes were conquered, kings captured, and Vespasian introduced by the fates.

14. *The southeastern part of the island was conquered and transformed into a province. When the governor Paulinus was campaigning in northwestern Wales, the province revolted.*

Aulus Plautius was the first of the consulars appointed governor and was succeeded by Ostorius Scapula, both of whom were distinguished in war; gradually the nearest part of Britain was reduced to the status of a province, with a colony of veterans added in addition.[17] Certain states were presented to King Togidumnus (he remained most faithful without a break up to our time) in accordance with an old and long-standing practice of the Roman people, to use even kings as tools of slavery. Then Didius Gallus maintained what had been won by his predecessors; he advanced only a few forts into the farther districts, and thereby sought the renown of having extended the province. Ve-

[17] *Camulodunum* (Colchester) was colonized under Ostorius.

ranius succeeded Didius, but died within a year. Then Suetonius Paulinus had great success for two years, subduing tribes
and establishing strong garrisons; because of his confidence in
his achievements, he attacked the island of Mona on the grounds
that it furnished strength to rebels and thus left his rear open to
opportunity for revolt.

15. *In Paulinus' absence, the Britons considered their injuries and the
small number of Rome's soldiers. The time was ripe to expel them from
the island.*

For, when fear was removed by the absence of the governor, the
Britons discussed among themselves the evils of slavery, compared their injuries, and made them seem worse by their interpretation of them: that nothing was gained by enduring them
except that more grievous injunctions were put upon them in
the belief that they were men who easily bore them. Once they
had had single kings, now two were put over them; the governor
was violent against their persons and the procurator against
their property. The rivalry and agreement of those put over
them were equally destructive to the subjects. The agents of
one, centurions, and of the other, slaves, mingled violence and
insults. Nothing was now safe from their greed, nothing from
their lust. In battle it is the stronger who plunders: now, as
things were, their homes were seized, their children dragged
off, levies imposed upon them as if their country was the only
thing for which they did not know how to die, by men who were
for the most part cowardly and unwarlike. For how small was
the number of soldiers who had come there if the Britons should
take a muster of themselves! It was in this way that the Ger-
manies had shaken off the yoke; and yet they were protected by
a river, not by the ocean. They, the Britons, had country, wives,
parents as reasons for war, the Romans had avarice and luxury.
The Romans would withdraw, as the deified Julius had with-
drawn, provided only that they copy the bravery of their ancestors. Nor should they be afraid because of the outcome of one
or two battles: the successful had more drive, but greater resolution was the possession of the wretched. Now even the gods,
who kept the Roman general away and the army far off on another island, were pitying the Britons; now they themselves
were taking counsel together, which had been the most difficult
thing. Besides, in undertakings of this kind, it was more dangerous to be caught than to dare.

16. *Under Boudicca, the Britons at first had great success, but were then destroyed by Paulinus. Peace and inactivity followed, as Rome was wracked by civil war.*

When they had aroused each other by these and similar remarks, with Boudicca, a woman of royal blood, as their leader (for they make no distinction of sex in their positions of command), they all began war; they went after the soldiers who were scattered in forts and then, when the garrisons had been stormed, attacked the colony itself as the capital of slavery, and anger and triumph omitted no kind of savagery found among barbarians. And unless Paulinus had quickly brought aid after hearing of the revolt of the province, Britain would have been lost. He restored it to its old submission by the favorable outcome of one battle, yet many men continued in arms, driven by their realization of their part in the uprising and by their personal fear of the governor, lest he, a man in other respects admirable, arrogantly pass judgment upon those who surrendered and with too great severity, as if avenging a personal affront. Petronius Turpilianus was therefore sent out, on the grounds that he was more compassionate and not involved in the crimes of the enemy and for this reason more inclined to receive repentance; after settling the old troubles, he dared nothing further and handed the province over to Trebellius Maximus. Trebellius, a more slothful man with no military experience, governed the province with a certain gentleness of administration. The barbarians now learned also to make allowance for attractive vices, and the intervention of civil wars furnished a legitimate excuse for inactivity; but trouble arose from mutiny, since the soldiers who were accustomed to campaigns grew wanton in peace. Trebellius, escaping the army's anger by flight and hiding, disgraced and without prestige, soon governed by sufferance; the license of the army was exacted, as it were, as the price of the general's safety, and the mutiny ended without bloodshed. Nor did Vettius Bolanus, since the civil wars still continued, disturb Britain with discipline: there was the same inactivity toward the enemy, similar violence in the camps, except for the fact that Bolanus, a man of integrity who was not hated for any misdeeds, had substituted affection for authority.

17. *When Vespasian became emperor, he appointed great generals as governor. Cerialis and Frontinus extended the territory of the province substantially.*

But when Vespasian recovered Britain along with the rest of the world, there followed great generals, magnificent armies, the diminishing of enemy hopes. And Petilius Cerialis at once brought terror by attacking the state of the Brigantes, which is said to be the most populous of the entire province. There were many battles, and sometimes they were not bloodless; and he embraced a large part of the Brigantes either in his victory or his war. And indeed Cerialis would have eclipsed the administration and reputation of any other successor, but Julius Frontinus, a great man as far as one could be great, took over and met the challenge, and reduced by arms the powerful and warlike tribe of the Silures, having overcome the difficulties of terrain as well as the bravery of the enemy.

Chapters 18–38. Agricola's seven years as governor.

18. *Agricola arrives in Britain late in the summer of 77. He wages an unexpected campaign successfully and gains great renown.*

This was the state of Britain, these the vicissitudes of wars that Agricola found, after having crossed over with summer already half gone, when the soldiers, on the ground that a campaign was out of the question, were turning to relaxed discipline and the enemy to taking advantage of the opportunity. Not long before his arrival, the state of the Ordovices had almost completely wiped out a cavalry unit that was stationed in their territory, and the province was aroused by this first step. Those who wished war approved the precedent and awaited the reaction of the new governor. Although summer was far gone, his detachments were scattered throughout the province, an end of campaigning for that year was assumed among the soldiery, circumstances that delay and are disadvantageous for a person intending to begin war, and it seemed more proper to many that the endangered areas be protected, Agricola decided to meet the crisis head on. After he had gotten together detachments of the legions and a small band of the auxiliaries, since the Ordovices did not dare to descend to the level plain, he led his troops up the hill, himself at the head of the column, so that the rest might have equal courage to face similar danger. And, when he had destroyed almost the entire tribe, realizing full well that one must follow up his reputation and that there would be terror for the rest in accordance with the outcome of first enterprises, he decided to reduce to his power the island of Mona, from the occupation of which I related above Paulinus had been recalled by the revolt of all Britain. But, since his plans were extemporized, ships were lacking: the skill and resolution of the general got the

troops across. Laying aside all the baggage, he launched picked
auxiliaries—who knew how to find fords and who had native
skill in swimming, by which they control themselves, their arms,
and horses simultaneously—into the water so suddenly that the
enemy, thunderstruck, who were expecting a fleet and ships
and an invasion by sea, believed that nothing was too difficult or
impossible for men who came to battle in this way. And so,
when they had sought peace and surrendered the island, Agricola was considered famous and great, since hard work and danger had been his choice on his entry into his province, a time
that others pass in display and the quest for popularity. Nor did
Agricola take advantage of the successful outcome of events for
personal gratification, or call keeping conquered peoples under
control an expedition or a victory; he did not even report his
achievements in wreathed dispatches,[18] but increased his renown by his concealment of renown, since people thought what
great hope for the future had been behind his silence about
achievements so great.

19. *He makes Rome's administration more acceptable by his personal
integrity and the elimination of abuses.*

But, judicious with regard to the province's feelings, and at the
same time taught by the experiences of others that too little was
accomplished by arms if injustice followed, he decided to elimi-
nate the causes of wars. Beginning with himself and his subordi-
nates, he first kept his own household in check, a task no less
difficult for many than to govern a province. No public business
was performed by freedmen and slaves, nor did he promote to
his staff a centurion or soldiers on the basis of personal prejudice or upon recommendation or entreaties, but he considered
each best man the most reliable. He knew everything, he did not
follow everything up. He pardoned small transgressions, he reserved his severity for large ones; he was sometimes content
with punishment, more often with repentance; he preferred to
put incorruptible men in charge of administration rather than to
condemn them after they had done wrong. He made the ex-
action of grain and tributes more endurable by equalizing the
burdens, having eliminated those tricks which, introduced for
profit, were more intolerable than the tribute itself. For the Britons were farcically compelled to take their stand by closed granaries and actually to buy the grain and satisfy their debt with

---

[18]Dispatches sent to Rome that reported military victories were wreathed with
laurel.

money; tortuous routes and far-off regions were assigned them, so that states would carry their grain into areas distant and lacking roads although winter camps were nearby, until what was easy for all became a source of profit for a few.[19]

20. *On campaign, Agricola led by example and by honorable treatment of the enemy induced many to surrender to Rome's rule.*

By putting an end to these things at once in his first year, he gave great repute to peace, which used to be feared no less than war because of the unconcern or the arrogance of his predecessors. But when summer came, after the army had been brought together, he was everywhere on the march, he praised discipline, he rebuked the disorderly; he himself chose the site for the camp, he himself reconnoitered estuaries and forests; and in the meantime he gave the enemy no relaxation, but kept on plundering them with sudden attacks; and when he had terrified them sufficiently, he showed them in contrast the inducements of peace by sparing them. Because of these actions, many states which up to that day had acted from a position of equality gave hostages and put aside their opposition, and were ringed round with garrisons and forts, with such great planning and care that no new part of Britain before this had come over to us with as little loss.

21. *He encouraged the activities of peace and civilization.*

The following winter was devoted to very profitable enterprises. For, in order that men who were scattered and uncivilized and for this reason easily moved to wars might become accustomed to peace and quiet through pleasures, he encouraged individuals and assisted communities to build temples, fora, and homes by praising those who were forward and rebuking those who were inactive. Thus competition for honor took the place of compulsion. Furthermore, he educated the sons of chieftains in the liberal arts and gave higher marks to the talents of the Britons than to the studied skill of the Gauls, with the result that those who recently rejected the Latin language desired eloquence. Then too our manner of dress became stylish and there

---

[19]The abuse was twofold. When grain was scarce, the Britons purchased it from the Romans to satisfy the terms of tribute. This grain, already in Roman granaries, never was removed, but money changed hands. When grain was plentiful, communities were required to deliver their quotas to places far away and difficult to reach, although Roman camps were in their vicinity. Then bribery was necessary to gain release from this absurd requirement.

was widespread use of the toga; and gradually they gave in to the attractions of vices, porticoes and baths and the elegance of banquets. And this was called civilization among those who did not know better, although it was part of slavery.

22. *The campaigns pushed farther to the north. Agricola established forts which were never stormed. The enemy had no success in either summer or winter.*

The third year of campaigns opened up new peoples, with tribes being laid waste as far as the Taus,[20] which is the name of the estuary. The enemy, overawed by such dread, did not dare to attack the army although it was struck by savage storms; there was even time to establish forts. Experienced men noted that no other general had chosen advantageous sites with greater good sense; no fort established by Agricola was either stormed by the enemy or abandoned by negotiations or retreat; for they were stocked with supplies to last a year against periods of siege. Thus winter there was uneventful, there were numerous sallies and each post defended itself; the enemy accomplished nothing and lost heart for this reason, because they had generally been accustomed to balance the losses of the summer with winter's profits but now were beaten in summer and winter alike. Nor did Agricola ever greedily claim for himself the deeds of others; whether centurion or prefect, a man had in him an honest witness of his achievement. He was reported by certain people to have been too harsh in his censures, and indeed, as he was kindly to the good, so was he unpleasant toward the bad. But no traces of his anger remained hidden away, so that one did not have to fear his silence: he considered it more honorable to give offense than to hate.

23. *The fourth year was devoted to the consolidation of the conquered land.*

The fourth summer was devoted to consolidating what he had overrun; and, if the army's bravery and the glory of the Roman name would permit, a boundary would have been found in Britain itself. For the Clota and the Bodotria,[21] carried far inland by the tides of the opposite seas, are separated by a narrow strip of land; this was then made secure with garrisons and the entire

---

[20] This is the river Tay.
[21] The Clyde and the Forth.

stretch of land to the south was occupied, with the enemy driven, as it were, onto another island.

24. *Continuing into Scotland, Agricola considered the advantages of the conquest of Ireland.*

In the fifth year of campaigns, having crossed over in the first ship,[22] he defeated tribes unknown up to that time in many successful battles; and he garrisoned that part of Britain that faces Ireland, with hope for the future rather than because of fear, since Ireland, situated between Britain and Spain and convenient also to the Gallic sea, would make a flourishing part of the empire a complete whole, with great mutual advantages. Its area, if compared to Britain, is smaller, but it is larger than the islands of our sea. Its soil and climate and the characters and civilization of its inhabitants differ little from those of Britain; its points of entry and harbors are known through trade and traders.[23] Agricola had given refuge to one of the princes of the people who had been driven out by internal revolt, and kept him with him under guise of friendship to use if the opportunity appeared. I often heard from Agricola that Ireland could be conquered and held by one legion and a small number of auxiliaries; and that this would be advantageous even with regard to Britain, if Roman arms were everywhere and liberty were, so to speak, removed from sight.

25. *On the advance further north, he made simultaneous use of army and navy. An attack by the Caledonians caused fear among some Romans, but Agricola chose to meet the enemy.*

But in the summer, in which he began the sixth year of his governorship, having included in his plans the states beyond the Bodotria, since uprisings of all the tribes beyond and threatening movements of the enemy army[24] were feared, he explored the harbors with his fleet; this was used by Agricola as part of his power and followed along with excellent effect, since war was carried forward simultaneously on land and sea, and often the infantry and cavalry and the sailors, in the same camp, sharing their supplies and pleasure, one by one exaggerated their

---

[22]This meaning of the words *nave prima transgressus* seems to be the best of a variety of poor versions. The text may well be corrupt.

[23]I choose to omit *in melius*.

[24]I prefer the reading *hostili exercitu* to Delz's *hostibus exercitus*.

own deeds and dangers, and at one moment the vastness of the forests and mountains, at another the dangers of storms and waves, on one side the conquest of land and enemy, on the other the conquest of the ocean were compared with soldierly boasting. The appearance of the fleet also astounded the Britons, as was heard from captives, on the ground that the last refuge for the conquered was closed, since the secret of their sea had been laid open. The inhabitants of Caledonia, peoples who had made great preparations, which were reported to be even greater, as usually happens about things that are unknown, having turned to military operations, undertook on their own accord to attack a fort, and the fact that they took the initiative had added to our fear; cowards, under the guise of judicious men, advised retreat back across the Bodotria and withdrawal in preference to being driven back; in the meantime Agricola learned that the enemy was going to attack in several columns. And, to prevent being surrounded by their superior numbers and because of their knowledge of the terrain, he advanced after he had himself divided his army into three parts.

26. *The enemy attacks a legion in its camp. Agricola comes to the rescue.*

When this became known to the enemy, they suddenly changed their plan and attacked the Ninth Legion, since it was particularly weak, by night with all their forces, and, after slaughtering the sentinels, burst upon them as they were terrified in their sleep. And fighting was now going on in the camp itself, when Agricola, informed of the enemy's march by scouts and following upon their footsteps, ordered the swiftest of the cavalry and infantry to fall upon their rear as they were fighting, and soon ordered the rest of the forces to add their battle cry; and the standards glistened in the dawn's light. The Britons were thus terrified by the double danger; and the men of the Ninth Legion recovered their spirit, and, sure of their safety, fought for glory. Even more, they turned to the attack, and there was a bitter fight in the narrow passageways of the gates themselves until the enemy were beaten, with the two armies rivaling one another, the one in order to seem to have brought assistance, the other to seem not to have needed aid. And had not swamps and forests furnished those who fled with cover, the war would have been brought to an end by that victory.

27. *Both sides are confident of ultimate success.*

The army, emboldened by their self-esteem and the renown of

this success, kept shouting that nothing could resist their bravery and that they should go right through Caledonia and at last,
with a continual series of battles, find the boundary of Britain.
And those who had just been cautious and wise were eager and
boastful after the event. This is the most unfair aspect of warfare: everybody claims successes for himself, while misfortunes
are charged to one person. But the Britons, having thought that
they had been overcome not by bravery, but by the skill of the
general in taking advantage of an opportunity, did not relax
their arrogance at all, but kept arming their young men, moving
their wives and children to safe places, and ratifying the conspiracy of states by meetings and sacrifices. And thus they parted
with inflamed spirits on both sides.

28. *The remarkable exploits of the Usipi, who revolt against their officers and escape by sailing around Britain.*

In the same summer, a cohort of the Usipi, who had been con-
scripted in the German provinces and had been sent to Britain,
dared a great and remarkable undertaking. After they had slain
a centurion and the soldiers who, assigned to their units to in-
still discipline, served as examples and instructors, they boarded
three light ships, and violently impressed their helmsmen; and,
with one of them setting the course[25] when the other two had
become suspect and had therefore been killed, since report of
them had not yet gotten abroad, they sailed along just like ghost
ships. Soon, when they had gone onto land to get water and
things they needed,[26] they fought battles with many of the Britons who defended their property and were often victorious, yet
sometimes driven off, and at last they came to such need that
they cannibalized their weakest and then those who had been
drawn by lot. And they sailed around Britain in this way, then,
with their ships lost as a result of lack of skill in navigating and
being considered pirates, they were cut off first by the Suebi,
then by the Frisii. And there were some whom the testimony of
such a great adventure made renowned, after they had been
sold into slavery in routine trade and had been brought as far as
our bank of the Rhine by passing from master to master.

[25]The reading of the text *uno remigante* is very difficult and has long been suspect; but, to my mind, none of the suggested emendations is any better. I prefer
therefore to keep the manuscript reading, in the sense that only one of the three
helmsmen did as he was told. We must then assume that he died, although this
is not stated, because, later in this chapter, Tacitus comments that ships were
lost because they lacked a pilot's skill.

[26]I read *utilia* rather than Delz's *utensilia*.

29. *The Romans advance to Mount Graupius, in the north of Scotland, to find thirty thousand of the enemy awaiting them.*

In the beginning of the following summer, Agricola, struck by a personal blow, lost the son who had been born the year before. He bore this misfortune neither with affectation as many brave men do nor again like a woman with lamentations and grief; and war was one of the remedies in his mourning. And so, sending his fleet ahead, which produced great and vague dread by plundering in many places, and with the army, to which he added those Britons who were the bravest and had been tested by long peace, stripped of heavy baggage, he came to Mount Graupius,[27] where the enemy had already taken up position. For the Britons, by no means disheartened by the outcome of the earlier battle and anticipating either revenge or slavery, and at last taught that a common danger must be beaten back in common, had summoned the strength of all states by embassies and alliances. And now more than thirty thousand armed men were in view, and there were still pouring in all the men of military age and the old men whose age was fresh and green, famous in war and each wearing his decorations, when a man named Calgacus, who among many leaders was preeminent in bravery and ancestry, is said to have addressed the gathered multitude, as they demanded battle, in words to this effect:

30. *Calgacus, leader of the Caledonians, arouses their spirits by invoking the evils of Roman rule.*

"As often as I consider the causes of war and our dire straits, I have great confidence that this day and your union will be the beginning of freedom for all Britain; for you have all joined together, you who have not experienced slavery, for whom there are no lands further on and not even the sea is safe, with the Roman fleet threatening us. Thus battle and weapons, which are honorable for the brave, are likewise the greatest source of safety even for cowards. Earlier struggles, in which we fought against the Romans with varying success, had a hope of assistance at our hands, since we, the noblest people of all Britain and for that reason living in its innermost sanctuary and not gazing upon any shores of those in slavery, kept our eyes also free from the contagion of conquest. Since we are the most distant people of the earth and of liberty, our very isolation and the obscurity of

[27]Some scholars now identify Mons Graupius with Bennachie northwest of Aberdeen.

our renown have protected us up to this day; now the farthest boundary of Britain lies open, and everything unknown is considered marvelous, but now there are no people further on, nothing except waves and rocks, and the Romans more hostile than these, whose arrogance you would in vain try to avoid by obedience and submission. Plunderers of the world, after they, laying everything waste, ran out of land, they search out the sea: if the enemy is wealthy, they are greedy; if he is poor they seek prestige; men whom neither the East nor the West has sated, they alone of all men desire wealth and poverty with equal enthusiasm. Robbery, butchery, rapine they call empire by euphemisms, and when they produce a wasteland, they call it peace.

31. *The conquered suffer continually; the earlier uprising of Boudicca was almost successful.*

"Nature has willed that a person's children and relatives be most precious to each one: these are carried off by levies to be slaves somewhere else; even if our wives and sisters have escaped the lust of enemies, they are defiled by men posing as friends and guests. Our property and fortunes are wasted for tribute, our land and its annual produce to provide grain, our very bodies and hands in laying roads through woods and swamps while suffering blows and insults. Slaves born to slavery are sold once and for all, and, in the bargain, are supported by their masters: Britain buys its slavery every day, she feeds it every day. And, just as in a household the newest slave is a butt of jokes for his fellow slaves, so, in this long-standing servitude of the world, we, new and unimportant, are sought for destruction; for we do not have fields or mines or harbors for the working of which we may be preserved. Further, bravery and independent spirit on the part of subjects are displeasing to conquerors; and as distance and isolation itself produce greater safety, so are they subject to greater suspicion. Thus, at last, put aside hope of pardon and take courage, whether safety or glory is most precious to you. The Brigantes,[28] under the leadership of a woman, were able to burn a colony to the ground and storm a camp, and could have thrown off the yoke if good fortune had not turned them to inactivity. We, who are at full strength and unconquered and on the verge of advancing to liberty and not repentance, let us right off, at the first clash, show the kind of men Caledonia has reserved for herself.

[28] The Brigantes took no part in the uprising.

32. *The Romans are inferior in numbers and valor. This is the last chance for freedom.*

"Or do you believe that the Romans have the same valor in war as wantonness in peace? Famous because of our disputes and disagreements, they turn the shortcomings of the enemy to the glory of their own army. As prosperity maintains this army, which is made up of the most diverse peoples, so will adversity destroy it, unless you suppose that Gauls and Germans and (I am ashamed to say it) many Britons—although they put their blood at the disposal of another's tyranny, yet they were enemies for a longer time than they have been slaves—are held by faith and affection. Fear and terror are weak bonds of devotion; as soon as you have removed these, those who have ceased to fear will begin to hate. All the inducements of victory are on our side: no wives encourage the Romans, no parents are going to reproach flight; many of them have no country, or a different one. Few in number, frightened because of what they do not know, anxiously gazing at the sky itself and the sea and the forests, which are all unknown, the gods have handed them over to you as if imprisoned and hypnotized. Do not be frightened by their delusive appearance nor the flash of gold and silver, which neither protects nor wounds. We shall find our allies in the enemies' very battle line: the Britons will recognize that our cause is theirs, the Gauls will recall their former freedom, the rest of the Germans will desert them just as much as recently the Usipi left them. Nor is there any source of dread behind them: there are deserted forts, colonies of old men, towns weak and suffering from disputes between unreliable subjects and unjust masters. Here is a general, here an army; there are tributes and mines and the other punishments of slaves; the decision to endure these forever or to avenge them at once rests upon this field. Therefore, think of your ancestors and your descendants as you go into battle."

33. *Agricola reminds the Romans that they have beaten their enemy in the past frequently and have advanced farther than any previous army.*

They received his speech with enthusiasm, signifying it, as is the custom for barbarians, with a roar and chant and discordant shouts. And now there were moving columns and flashes of weapons as all the most daring men dashed forth; at the same time the line of battle was being drawn up, when Agricola, thinking that his soldiers, although confident and scarcely restrained by the fortifications, should still be harangued, spoke as follows:

"This is the seventh year, fellow soldiers, from the time you began to conquer Britain by your bravery, the auspices of the Roman Empire, and my loyal assistance. In so many campaigns, in so many battles, whether there was need of bravery against the enemy or endurance and hard work almost against nature herself, I have not had any regrets about my troops nor you about your general. Therefore we have gone beyond the limits, I of the governors of old, you of former armies, and we occupy the farthest part of Britain, not by rumor or report, but with a camp and arms: Britain has been discovered and subdued. Often, indeed, on the march, when swamps or mountains and rivers were wearing you out, I heard the words of every very brave individual: 'When will the enemy be given to us, when the battle?' They are coming, flushed out of their lairs, and your prayers and prowess have a free field, and everything is easy if you win but difficult if you lose. For, just as the accomplishment of so great a march, the conquest of forests, the crossing of estuaries are splendid and glorious as one goes forward, so are those circumstances that are today most lucky the source of very great danger for men in flight; for we do not have the same knowledge of the terrain or the same abundance of supplies, but armed forces and on these rests everything. As far as I am concerned, I decided long ago that the backs neither of an army nor of a general were safe. Therefore not only is an honorable death preferable to a life of disgrace, but safety and renown are inseparable; nor would it be without glory to have fallen at the very limit of land and of the world.

34. *Now is the chance for final victory, which will make all Britain Roman.*

"If new tribes and an unknown army had taken up position, I should encourage you by the precedents of other armies: as it is, review your own glories, question your own eyes. These are the men whom you overwhelmed with a shout last year when they had attacked one legion under cover of night; these men are the most given to flight when compared with the rest of the Britons, and for this reason they have survived so long. Just as all the bravest animals rushed against you as you passed through woods and groves and the cowardly and slothful were driven off by the very sound of the column, so the fiercest of the Britons have

long since fallen, what is left is a mass of unwarlike cowards. As
to the fact that you have at last found them, they have not made
a stand, but they have been caught; dire extremity and shock
from great fear have fixed their line of battle on this ground,
where you are to produce a beautiful and splendid victory. Be
done with campaigns, cap fifty years with one great day, prove
to the commonwealth that delays of war or causes of revolt
could never have been charged to the army."

35. *The two armies take their positions. Agricola posts himself before
the standards.*

The enthusiasm of the soldiers became obvious while Agricola
was still speaking and great eagerness followed the end of his
address, and they immediately rushed to their arms. He de-
ployed them, afire and eager to attack, in such a way that the
auxiliaries of infantry, which numbered eight thousand, made
the center of the line strong and the three thousand cavalry were
spread out on the flanks. The legions were stationed before the
rampart, since it would be a great glory of victory to have waged
the war without shedding Roman blood, and as reinforcement,
if the others should be beaten. The line of the Britons had taken
its stand on higher ground for show as well as to induce terror in
this way: the first rank was on level ground, the rest, stationed
close together, rose, as if it were, one above the other up the
sloping ridge; the chariot cavalry filled the plain between with
the noise of their dashing back and forth. Then Agricola, fearing
that fighting would occur simultaneously on his front and flanks
since the number of the enemy was far greater than his own,
spread his ranks, although the battle line was going to be too
extended and many advised that the legions should be brought
into play, and himself, more inclined toward hope and stalwart
against adversity, sent his horse away and took his position as a
foot-soldier before the standards.

36. *After initial success, the enemy is driven back.*

And at the first encounter fighting was carried on at long range;
the Britons, with resolution and skill, knocked aside the javelins
of our men with their huge swords or shook them loose from
their small shields, and they themselves sent over a tremendous
barrage of weapons, until Agricola urged on the four cohorts of
Batavians and the two of the Tungri to bring the battle to sword's
point hand to hand; they were skilled in this by their long expe-

rience in military service and it was difficult for the enemy; for the swords of the Britons, lacking a point, did not withstand the crossing of weapons and battle at close quarters. Therefore, when the Batavians began to inflict blows in great numbers, to strike with their shieldbosses, to dig at their enemies' faces, and, when those who had been stationed on level ground had been cut down, to move their line up onto the hills, the rest of the cohorts, exerting full effort in emulation and attack, slew those who were nearest to them, and many were left behind half dead or unwounded in the haste for victory. In the meantime, the squadrons of cavalry, when the charioteers fled, joined the infantry battle. And although they had inflicted fresh terror, nonetheless they could not move freely in the midst of the thick ranks of the enemy and on the uneven ground; and it hardly looked like a cavalry engagement, since those who kept their footing with difficulty on the slope were pushed by the bodies of the horses; and often uncontrolled chariots and riderless horses, which had been terrified, ran through their ranks from the flanks or front as fright had driven each on.

37. *British reinforcements are repelled and a rout ensues. The Romans gain a total victory.*

And the Britons, who, taking no part so far in the fight, had occupied the tops of the hills and were, without apprehension, scorning the small number of our men, began gradually to come down and would have begun to surround the rear of the winning side if Agricola, fearing that very move, had not placed in their path four cavalry units that had been kept in reserve for emergencies, and if, as they had attacked with greater ferocity, he had not caused them to flee, beaten all the more bitterly. In this way the plan of the Britons was turned upon themselves, and the horsemen, going beyond the line of battle by order of the general, attacked the line of the enemy from the rear. Then, indeed, there was a great and terrible scene on the open ground: the Romans undertook to pursue, to wound, to take captives, and to kill these when others were offered them. Now armed groups of the enemy, according to each man's inclination, fled before inferior numbers; some who were unarmed even charged forth and offered themselves to death. Everywhere there were weapons and bodies and mangled limbs, and the ground was bloody; and sometimes even the vanquished had fury and valor. For after they approached the woods, gathering together and knowing the locale, they ambushed the first pursuers who were incautious. And if Agricola, who was present everywhere, had not ordered strong and lightly equipped cohorts to advance as if in a hunt and, where the woods were thicker, part of the cavalry to advance unmounted and, where the woods were thinner, the cavalry to search in every direction, some loss would have been received because of overconfidence. But when the Britons saw that the Romans were again in pursuit, drawn up in orderly ranks, they turned in flight, not in groups, as before, nor with one having any regard for another: isolated and avoiding each other, they sought distant and trackless places. Night and satiation brought an end to pursuit. About ten thousand of the enemy were slain; three hundred sixty of our men fell, among whom was Aulus Atticus, prefect of a cohort, who had charged the enemy because of his youthful enthusiasm and the boldness of his horse.

38. *Enemy survivors are hunted down. The campaign ends and Agricola leads the army into winter quarters.*

And indeed night brought pleasure to the conquerors with rejoicing and booty; the Britons, scattering, with the mingled wailing of men and women, dragged their wounded along, summoned the uninjured, deserted their homes and with their own hands set them afire in anger, chose hiding places and immediately left them; they made some plans in common, then took them individually; sometimes they were crushed by the sight of their loved ones, more often driven to fury. And there was clear evidence that some laid violent hands on their wives and children as if they pitied them. The next day revealed more widely the appearance of victory: everywhere was overwhelming silence, desolate hills, houses smoking in the distance, no one found by the scouts. Agricola sent these off in every direction, and when it was learned that there were only random traces of flight and that the enemy was being marshaled nowhere, and that war could not be extended because summer was almost over, he led his army into the territory of the Boresti. There, when hostages had been received, he ordered the commander of the fleet to sail around Britain. Military forces were assigned for this purpose, and, besides, terror had cleared the way. He himself placed the infantry and cavalry in winter quarters, after a slow march, so that the spirits of the recently subdued tribes might be cowed by the very lack of haste of his journey. And at the same time the fleet, with favorable weather and reputation, occupied the harbor of Trucculum,[29] from which it reconnoitred the adjacent coast of Britain and to which it had returned without loss.

Chapters 39–43. Agricola's recall and last years.

39. *The report of Agricola's great victory causes Domitian concern.*

This sequence of events, although reported in Agricola's dispatches without exaggeration, Domitian received, as was his custom, with joyful appearance and anxious heart. He realized that his recent fake triumph over Germany had held him up to ridicule, when people had been purchased in trade whose appearance and hair were worked on to make them look like captives, but now a real and great victory was being celebrated with tremendous renown after so many thousands of the enemy had been slain. This was of particular concern to him, that the name of a subject was raised above the emperor's. In vain had public eloquence and the prestige of political careers been crushed and silenced, if someone else should lay claim to military glory; other talents were rather easily disregarded, one way or another, but to be a good general was the mark of an emperor. Disturbed by such cares and, what was an indication of his savage intent, having gotten his fill of seclusion,[30] he thought it best for the present to let his hatred ride, until the excitement caused by Agricola's popularity and the support of the army should wane; for at that very time Agricola held Britain.

40. *Agricola is voted all honors and recalled from Britain. He enters Rome at night and is modestly received by the emperor.*

Therefore he orders that the triumphal decorations and the compliment of a splendid statue and whatever is granted in place of a triumph, crowned with lengthy eulogy, be decreed in the senate and the impression be given in addition that the province of Syria, which then lacked a governor because of the death of the consular Atilius Rufus and which was reserved for men of the greatest distinction, was marked out for Agricola. Quite a few believed that a freedman from the emperor's private councils was sent to Agricola and carried an order in which Syria was assigned to him, with this instruction, that it should be transmitted if Agricola were still in Britain; that freedman met Agricola

---

[29] The location of the tribe of the Boresti and the harbor of Trucculum have not been identified.
[30] Domitian spent much time in isolation at his Alban villa.

on the English Channel, and returned to Domitian without having even addressed him. It is not known whether this is the truth or whether it was made up and designed in accord with the emperor's character. In the meantime, Agricola had handed over his province, at peace and secure, to his successor. And, that there might not be an entry into Rome that would be note-worthy by the great crowd of those who came to meet him, he entered the city at night, having avoided the attendance of friends, and came to the Palatine at night as had been ordered; and, received with a brief kiss and without a word, he lost him-self in the crowd of courtiers. But in order to balance his military reputation, which is unpopular among civilians, with other qualities, he drank deeply of quiet and rest, modest in demea-nor, affable in conversation, accompanied by one or at most two friends, to such an extent that many, whose custom it was to judge great men by their outward show, when they had seen and observed Agricola, inquired of his reputation, few inter-preted his modesty properly.

41. *His reputation brings him into danger with the emperor. Military disasters along the Danube cause the people to demand that he be given command, but he is ignored.*

During those days, he in his absence frequently had accusations leveled at him before Domitian, and in his absence was acquit-ted. The cause of his danger was not any charge or complaint of injury to anyone, but an emperor hostile to excellence, the man's renown, and the worst kind of enemies, those who praise. And indeed there followed the kinds of crises for the state that did not permit Agricola to be passed over in silence; so many armies were lost in Moesia and Dacia and Germany and Pannonia by the rash inexperience or cowardice of their generals, so many military men with so many cohorts had been assaulted and cap-tured; now the question was no longer about the boundary of the empire and the riverbank, but about the winter quarters of the legions and occupation of the provinces. Thus, when disas-ter was followed by disaster and every year was marked by deaths and defeats, Agricola was demanded as general by the voice of the common people, since all compared his activity, resolution, and experience in wars with the laziness and cowar-dice of the others. There is no doubt that Domitian's ears too were bombarded by these comments; while all the best freed-men kept influencing the emperor, who inclined to evil, out of affection and loyalty toward him, the worst did it out of ill will and jealousy toward Agricola. Thus Agricola was led headlong into that very glory simultaneously by his own good qualities and the vices of others.

42. *Agricola is warned not to seek the governorship of Asia or Africa. Yet his career showed that good men can exist under bad emperors.*

The year was now at hand in which lots would be cast for the proconsulship of Africa and Asia, and, since Civica[31] had recently been put to death, Agricola did not lack advice nor Domitian a precedent. Certain men who were privy to the emperor's thoughts approached Agricola, to ask him on their own whether he intended to go to a province. And at first they praised leisure and rest rather surreptitiously, soon they offered their services in supporting his refusal, at last, simultaneously urging and terrifying him, no longer hiding their intent, they dragged him to Domitian. The emperor, armed with hypocrisy and with an arrogant manner, heard Agricola's prayers to be excused and, when he had assented, allowed himself to be thanked, nor did he blush because of the hatefulness of his kindness. Nonetheless, he did not give Agricola the proconsular stipend which was customarily offered and which he himself had granted to certain individuals, whether he was angered that it had not been requested or from a pang of conscience, lest he seem to have purchased what he had forbidden. It is a characteristic of human nature to hate the person whom you have injured; indeed, Domitian's character inclined toward anger and it was the more inexorable as it was more concealed, yet he was appeased by Agricola's sense of proportion and insight, since he did not pursue renown and an untimely end by willful stubbornness and a useless display of liberty. Let those whose custom it is to admire actions that are forbidden know that great men can exist even under bad emperors; and allegiance and moderation, if hard work and vigorous action are added, can reach the same level of renown that many have reached by dangerous paths, but they became famous by an ostentatious death, with no advantage to the state.

43. *Agricola's death and the emperor's response.*

The end of his life was grievous to us, sad to his friends, a matter of concern even to those who had no contact with him and

---

[31]C Vettulenus Civica Cerialis, governor of Asia in 88–89, was killed for disloyalty to emperor Domitian.

those who did not know him. The common folk, too, and this indifferent people kept coming to his home and spoke of him in the fora and in private groups; nor did anyone, when Agricola's death was reported, rejoice or immediately forget him. And the continuing rumor that he had been cut off by poison increased their pity: I would not dare to state that any of this was proven to us. But it is true that, throughout the course of his illness, ranking freedmen and the emperor's personal physicians came more frequently than was to be expected from the custom of the principate, which made calls by means of messengers, whether that attention was solicitude or spying. Indeed, it was agreed that, on his last day, all the crises of his decline were reported by posted couriers, while no one believed that such haste would be devoted to matters that the emperor would hear in sadness. Nonetheless, Domitian displayed an appearance of emotional grief in his manner and expression, now undisturbed by his hatred and being the kind of man who could more easily conceal joy than fear. There was no doubt but that, when Agricola's will had been read, in which he appointed Domitian as joint heir with his most excellent wife and most devoted daughter, the emperor rejoiced as if intentionally honored. So blind and corrupted by constant flatteries was his mind that he did not realize that no one is designated heir by a good father except a bad emperor.

Chapters 44–46. Epilogue.

44. *Sketch of Agricola's life and character.*

Agricola was born on June 13, in the year of Gaius Caesar's third consulship; he died in his fifty-fourth year, on August 23, when Collega and Priscinus were consuls. But if posterity should also wish to learn of his appearance, he was well proportioned rather than tall; there was no trace of vehemence in his expression; rather there was a good deal of charm in his appearance. One would easily have believed him a good man, willingly a great one. And he himself indeed, although taken away in the midcourse of his prime, lived a very long life as far as glory is concerned. For he had fully enjoyed all the true goods that are based upon excellence, and what else could fortune add for a man who had been consul and had been honored with the decorations of a triumph? He did not get satisfaction from excessive wealth, but he had sufficient. Since his daughter and wife survive him, he can even seem blessed, because he escaped what was to come, with his rank unimpaired, his reputation secure, his relatives and friends uninjured. For, although it was not permitted him to live to see this light of a most happy age and Trajan as emperor, a circumstance that he used to forecast in our hearing with prophecy and prayers, yet he has as considerable compensation for his hastened death the fact that he escaped that last period, in which Domitian drained the state, no longer at intervals and with respites of time, but with, as it were, one continuous blow.

45. *By his death, Agricola escaped the sight of the senate under siege and many men put to death.*

Agricola did not see the senate house under siege and the senate ringed by arms and, in one and the same massacre, the murders of so many men of consular rank, the exiles and flights of so many very distinguished women. Mettius Carus was credited with only one triumph, Messalinus' violent opinion had influence only within the citadel at Alba, and Baebius Massa was already then a defendant.[32] Soon our hands led Helvidius to prison; the sight of Mauricus and Rusticus dishonored us, and Senecio drenched us with guiltless blood.[33] Nero at least withdrew his eyes and ordered his crimes but did not watch them; an especial part of misery under Domitian was to see and to be seen, when our sighs were noted down, when that savage face and ruddy expression, with which he fortified himself against shame, were able to mark out the paleness of so many men.

You were indeed fortunate, Agricola, not only in the fame of your life, but also by the timeliness of your death. As those who were present at your last words report, you received your end with constancy and serenity, as if you would grant the emperor acquittal as much as a man could. But his daughter and I, beyond the bitterness of losing a parent, are made even sadder by the fact that it was not our luck to attend his illness, comfort him in his decline, or get our fill of sight and embrace. We would certainly have caught his instructions and words, which we would fix deeply in our minds. This is our particular grief, this our

[32]Mettius Carus and Lucius Valerius Catullus Messalinus were notorious informers, Baebius Massa was prosecuted in 93 for misconduct while governor of the province of Baetica. The prosecutors were Pliny the Younger and Senecio.
[33]Helvidius Priscus was the son of the Helvidius mentioned in chapter 2. Mauricus and Rusticus were brothers. The former, banished by Domitian, was recalled by Nerva; the latter was put to death under Domitian along with Senecio. See chapter 2.

wound, that he was lost to us four years before, owing to the circumstances of so long an absence.[34] Unquestionably, best of parents, everything and more was done for your honor with your most devoted wife at your side; nonetheless, you were laid to rest with fewer tears, and at the last moment of light your eyes longed for something.

46. *If souls do survive death, may you rest in peace. Your achievements have gained you immortality.*

If there is any abode for the spirits of the good, if, as it pleases the philosophers, great souls are not extinguished together with the body, may you rest in peace, and may you summon us, your family, from weak yearning and womanly lamentations to consideration of your good qualities, which ought properly neither to be grieved over nor bewailed. Let us rather honor you with admiration and praises and, if nature permits, with emulation. This is true honor, this the devotion of all the nearest of kin. I should also give your daughter and wife this advice, to cherish the memory of father and husband in such a way as to ponder all his deeds and words, to embrace the appearance and aspect of his mind rather than of his body, not because I think one should do without the statues that are made of marble or bronze, but, as with the faces of men, so are the portraits of faces feeble and transitory, while the quality of the mind is immortal, which you could preserve and express not by another's material and skill, but by your own character. Whatsoever in Agricola we loved and admired, that remains and is going to remain in the minds of men, in the never-ending span of time, by the glory of his achievements; for oblivion will overwhelm many men of old as if they were without glory and of no rank: Agricola will survive, his story told and transmitted to posterity.

[34] Tacitus was absent from Rome from 89 to 93, serving, in all probability, as governor of a praetorian province or as commander of a legion.

Germany

The structure of the *Germany* is simple. The work falls naturally into two halves of almost equal length: the first considers, in general, the land and its people, their customs and practices in chapters 1 through 27; the second is concerned with the description of the individual tribes, in chapters 28 through 46. But each of these two main divisions can be broken down a bit further. The general treatment devotes the first five chapters to geographical description of the land and to the origin of the people; the next ten chapters deal with public institutions, the following twelve with those of private life. The public and private sections are almost precisely the same in length.

Tacitus' consideration of the individual tribes is not a random presentation. Chapters 28 through 37 deal with the tribes of the west and northwest, generally following the line of the Rhine from south to north. The remainder of the work covers the Suebic tribes of the east and north, generally following the course of the Danube from west to east before he jumps, as he must, to the almost fairy-tale lands of the far north. Again, both parts are treated at almost the same length, although the amount of detail that Tacitus can present gradually diminishes as he moves farther away from the parts of Germany well known to the Romans through warfare and commerce.

There are two passages that perhaps seem out of place in an ethnographical essay; they verge rather upon history. The first appears at the end of chapter 33, where Tacitus meditates upon the future of Rome's empire after he has reported the practically total annihilation of the Bructeri, an annihilation accomplished by other Germanic peoples without any involvement of the Romans, who looked upon the event as if watching games in the amphitheater. The interpretation of this passage, to gain insight into Tacitus' thoughts on historiography and Rome's survival, is briefly discussed in footnote 15 below.

The other is the long excursus (chapter 37) on Rome's two centuries and more of warfare and trial to conquer the Germans. Since the latter days of the second century B.C., Tacitus says, they have tested Rome's mettle and fought on equal terms with

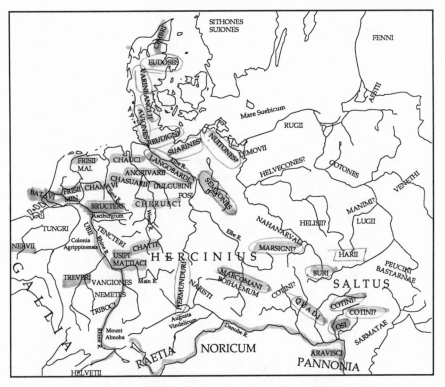

Germany in the time of Tacitus

her armies; the freedom of the Germans is a greater danger than
the royal dynasty of the Parthians, and no other enemy in time
past had proved so unconquerable. Indeed, although Tacitus
does no more than hint it, it may well be that the defeat inflicted
by Arminius, the first great national German hero, upon Varus
and his three legions in the Teutoburg Forest in A.D. 9 was the
most potent setback in Rome's history up to that time. Previous
disasters, such as the battle at the Caudine Forks against the
Samnites in 321 B.C., the battle at Cannae against Hannibal and
the Carthaginians in 216, and that at Arausio against the Cimbri
and Teutons in 105, only delayed the outcome in each instance;
Rome was, in a matter of years, ultimately victorious. But Varus'
overwhelming loss changed Roman foreign policy fundamen-
tally. The campaigns of Augustus' stepsons, Drusus and Ti-

berius, the later emperor, in the score of years on either side of the beginning of the Christian era, were intended to extend Rome's boundary against the unconquered tribes of Germany from the Rhine to the Elbe. After Varus' loss of his three legions, whose numbers XVII, XVIII, and XIX, never again appeared in the legionary rosters, Augustus became content with the Rhine frontier; and future operations against the Germans, as those by Domitian, were generally concerned rather with consolidation of this Rhine line by shortening the salient between the Rhine and the Danube and establishing a defended border known as the *limes*. Only Marcus Aurelius was to have a larger vision once again. Suetonius tells the pathetic story of Augustus wandering around his residence, repeating again and again, "Varus, Varus, give me back my legions" (*The Deified Augustus* 23.2). In chapter 37, Tacitus rises far above the level of ethnography with the insight and judgments of the true historian.

Tacitus had many predecessors in the composition of an ethnological study in which the writer undertook to explain the culture and peculiarities of people generally unknown to his audience. Among ancient writers Herodotus is surely the best known, for his long descriptions of Egypt and Scythia, a region now part of southern Russia. Of Tacitus' Roman antecedents, the most important is Sallust, the historian of the late republic, who was a model for him both in the approach to history and in its writing. In the monograph on the Numidian prince Jugurtha and his struggles against Rome, Sallust included an extensive excursus on the north African land and its people.

In his first essay, the *Agricola*, Tacitus could call upon the subject of the biography himself for information and insight. Such a source was unavailable for the *Germania*. Whatever his own experience in Germany had been, most of his information came from literary sources, above all Pliny the Elder, who had extensive service in both German provinces as well as in Gallia Belgica, immediately adjacent. It is even possible that Tacitus was able to interview the learned man himself.

Although the information was largely obtained from others, his own handling of his material is clear throughout. Some anachronisms, recalling the status of an earlier period, do exist, but the level of accuracy is again very high, confirmed by the findings of archaeology.

Whatever Tacitus' purpose in writing, one of the most striking aspects of the work is the respect shown for the Germans, whose lives and characters are described as purer and simpler than those of his contemporaries. The theme of the noble savage, whose simplicity is shown to be superior to Rome's higher civilization, is a commonplace in ancient writing. Civilization has many advantages, to be sure, but it tends to corrupt *mores*, the basic sense of what is right.

Germany

Chapters 1–5. Geographical description and origin of the people.

1. *Germany's boundaries.*

Germany as a whole is separated from the Gauls and the Rae-
tians and Pannonians by the Rhine and Danube rivers, from the
Sarmatians and the Dacians by mutual fear or mountains; the
ocean bounds the rest, embracing broad peninsulas and islands
of huge size, with certain tribes and kings, whom war revealed,
becoming known only in recent times. The Rhine, rising in an
inaccessible and precipitous height of the Raetian Alps, makes a
gentle sweep to the west and empties into the northern ocean.
The Danube, springing from a sloping and gently rising ridge of
Mount Abnoba, passes among a larger number of peoples, until
it bursts into the Pontic Sea in six channels; a seventh mouth is
lost in swamps.[1]

2. *The people are indigenous. Tradition about their origin varies; the
name "Germany" is not ancient.*

I should believe that the Germans themselves are indigenous
and have hardly been affected by the immigration of other
peoples and intercourse with them, since in time past those who
wished to change their living places did not travel by land but by
sea, and the ocean, immense beyond and, so to speak, hostile, is
rarely visited by ships from our world. Besides, not to speak of
the danger of a terrible and unknown sea, who would have left
Asia or Africa or Italy and sought Germany, which is rough in
terrain, bitter in climate, gloomy to live in and to see, unless it be
one's native land?

They relate in ancient songs, which is the only kind of historical tradition among them, that the god Tuisto was born from
earth. They assign him a son Mannus, the source and founder of
the race, and to Mannus three sons, from whose names those

[1] Whether the first words of the monograph, *Germania omnis*, were meant to
recall the beginning of Caesar's *Gallic War* or were part of stock ethnographical
vocabulary is a question that has been long and variously discussed. Mount Abnoba is in the Black Forest. The Pontic Sea is the Black Sea.

nearest the ocean are called Ingaevones, those in the center Herminones, the rest Istaevones. Certain sources claim, as customarily happens with the license of antiquity, that the god had more offspring and that there were more designations of the people, Marsi, Gambrivii, Suebi, Vandilii, and that these are the real and ancient names. But the name of Germany is recent and lately introduced, since those who were the first to cross the Rhine and drive out the Gauls and are now called the Tungri were then called the Germani: so gradually the name of a tribe, not of a people, prevailed, with the result that all the people, at first called Germani by the victorious tribe in order to inject fear in the Gauls, soon gave themselves the same name after it had been invented.[2]

3. *Hercules and Ulysses are said to have visited Germany. The importance among the Germans of the war cry.*

There is the report that Hercules too spent time among them and, when ready to go into battle, they sing of him as the bravest of all brave men. They also have songs of this kind, by the recitation of which (they call it *barditus*, or war cry) they rouse their courage, and they forecast the outcome of the coming fight from the sound alone; for they cause terror or are themselves afraid, depending upon the shout of the battle line, and the sounds seem not so much voices as a chorus of bravery. Harshness and the intermittent roar of sound are particularly aimed at by putting their shields to their mouths, so that a richer and deeper tone may swell from the echo. But certain authorities think that Ulysses too, in that long and fabled wandering of his, was carried into this ocean and came to the lands of Germany, and that Asciburgium, which is located on the bank of the Rhine and inhabited even today, was founded by him and called Askipurgion: they claim further that an altar, dedicated by Ulysses with his father Laertes' name added, was once found in the same place, and that monuments and certain mounds, with Greek inscriptions upon them, still exist on the boundary of Germany and Raetia. It is not my intent to support these statements with proofs or to refute them: let each person believe or disbelieve according to his inclination.

[2]"This is one of the most disputed sentences in Latin literature" (Anderson). It has inspired many attempts to clarify the meaning by revising the text. Yet I think that Tacitus' meaning is clear although the latter part of the sentence is contorted because of its very concision.

[handwritten margin note: Hercules maybe but Ulysses, no!]

cynical *no*

4. *The Germans are a unique race, unpolluted by intermarriages.*

I personally incline to the views of those who think that the peoples of Germany have not been polluted by any marriages with other tribes and that they have existed as a particular people, pure and only like themselves. As a result, all have the same bodily appearance, as far as is possible in so large a number of men: fiery blue eyes, red hair, large bodies which are strong only for violent exertion. There is no comparable endurance of hardship and labors and they do not endure thirst and heat at all, but they have become accustomed to cold and hunger from their climate and soil.

5. *Characteristics of the land. The Germans' unconcern for precious metals.*

Although the land is somewhat varied in appearance, nonetheless on the whole it is gloomy with forests or unwholesome with swamps, damper where it faces the Gauls, windier where it faces Noricum and Pannonia; it is fertile for grain crops, does not bear fruit trees, and is rich in livestock, but the animals are generally small. Not even the cattle have their natural beauty or pride of brow: the Germans delight in number, and these are their only form of wealth, as well as being highly prized. I do not know whether the gods in their kindness or anger have denied them silver and gold. Yet I would not claim that no vein of Germany produces silver or gold: for who has searched? They are not influenced by the possession and use of the precious metals as much as one might expect. For one can see among them that silver vessels, given as gifts to their ambassadors and chieftains, are considered no more valuable than those made out of clay; nonetheless, those nearest our border value gold and silver for commercial purposes and recognize and prefer certain types of our money: those farther away from us make use of barter in a simpler and more ancient manner. They like money that is ancient and long known, notched silver coins and coins stamped with a two-horse chariot. They favor silver more than gold, not from any predilection, but because the number of silver coins is easier to use for those who trade in common and cheap items.

Chapters 6–15. Public institutions.

6. *Weapons and mode of fighting.*

Not even iron is found in abundance, as is inferred from the character of their weapons. Very few use swords or lances of great size: they wield spears or, as they call them, *frameae*, with a narrow and short iron point, but so sharp and easy to use that they fight with the same weapon either at close range or at a distance, as circumstance requires. And the horseman, indeed, is satisfied with a shield and a *framea;* the foot soldiers also hurl light weapons, each individual more than one, and they throw them a great distance, naked or lightly garbed with a cloak. There is no show in their appearance; they only decorate their shields with the choicest colors. Few have breastplates, scarcely one or two have helmets made of metal or of leather. Their horses are not outstanding either in appearance or in speed. But they are also not trained to vary wheeling maneuvers after our fashion: the Germans drive their horses straight ahead or with a single sweep to the right, with the line so well disciplined that no one falls behind. When one considers them on the whole, they have greater strength in their infantry; and for this reason they fight in battle with mixed forces, with the running speed of the infantry appropriate and suitable for a cavalry encounter; these infantrymen, chosen from all the young men, they station before the battle line. And their number is precisely defined: there are one hundred from each canton, and this is their very name, the "Hundredmen," among their own people, and what was at first a number is now a title and an honor. The battle line is disposed in wedge-shaped units. They consider retreat a mark of prudence rather than of terror, provided you press on again. They recover the bodies of their own even in battles where success is doubtful. To have abandoned one's shield is the greatest crime, nor is it right for one so disgraced to be present at religious ceremonies or to enter the council, and many who have survived wars ended their disgrace by hanging themselves.

7. *The power of kings, generals, and priests. The importance of families and clans.*

They pick their kings on the basis of noble birth, their generals on the basis of bravery. Nor do their kings have limitless or arbitrary power, and the generals win public favor by the example they set if they are energetic, if they are distinguished, if they fight before the battle line, rather than by the power they wield. But no one except the priests is allowed to inflict punishment with death, chains, or even flogging, and the priests act not, as it were, to penalize nor at the command of the general, but, so to speak, at the order of the god, who they believe is at hand when they are waging war. And so they bear into battle certain images and emblems that have been removed from sacred groves; and, what is a particular incitement to bravery, neither chance nor a miscellaneous grouping brings about the cavalry or infantry formation, but families and clans; and close by are their dear ones, whence are heard the wailings of women and the crying of children. These are each man's most sacred witnesses, these are his greatest supporters: it is to their mothers and to their wives that they bring their wounds; and the women do not quake to count or examine their blows, and they furnish sustenance and encouragement to the fighters.

8. *The impact and influence of women.*

It is recorded that some battle lines, when already broken and giving way, were restored by the women, by persistent prayers and showing their breasts and pointing to the nearness of captivity, which the Germans fear much more violently for the sake of their women, to such a degree that the spirits of states are more effectively kept under control when the latter are ordered to include girls of high birth among hostages. They even think that there is a sacred and prophetic quality in women, and so they neither reject their advice nor scorn their forecasts. We saw that, under the deified Vespasian, Veleda was for a long time considered a divinity by many; but in time past they also worshipped Aurinia and several others, not because of fawning nor as if to make them goddesses.

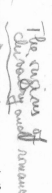

9. *The chief gods and the manner of worship.*

Of the gods they worship Mercury above all, whom they consider it right on specific days to propitiate with human as well as other sacrifices. They win the favor of Hercules and Mars[3] with animals suitable for the purpose. Some of the Suebi sacrifice also to Isis: I have been unable to find out whence the cause and origin of a foreign rite came, except that the symbol itself, fashioned in the shape of a ship, tells of a religion that was imported. But, in keeping with the greatness of divinities, they think it proper neither to confine their gods within walls nor to give them any likeness of human appearance: they consecrate groves and glades and call by the names of gods that intangible quality they see with the eye of reverence alone.

[3]Tacitus uses Roman names for local German deities.

10. *The importance of prophecy; the varied means of ascertaining the future.*

They have as much regard as anyone for auspices and the taking of lots. Their method of casting lots is unvaried. They slice a branch cut from a fruit tree into slips and throw these, distinguished by certain marks, completely at random onto a white cloth. Then the priest of the state, if it is a public consultation, or the head of the family, if it is private, first having prayed to the gods and gazing up at the sky, picks up three, one at a time, and interprets them in accordance with the mark that had been inscribed before. If the lots have forbidden anything, there is no consultation about the same subject on the same day; but if permission has been won, the support of the auspices is still required. And the following indeed is known even here, to make inquiry of the sounds and flights of birds; it is a distinctive characteristic of the race also to make trial of the forebodings and warnings of horses. The horses are raised at public expense in the same glades and groves,[4] all white and unpolluted by any work for man; when they have been yoked to a sacred chariot, the priest and the king or the chief of the state accompany them and observe their neighings and snortings. And greater credence is given to no other method of prophecy, and not only among the common people but also among the aristocracy and among the priests; for the latter consider that they are servants of the gods while the horses are privy to the gods' thoughts. There is also another method for taking auspices, whereby they forecast the outcome of serious wars. They match a man of that tribe with which they are at war, captured in some way or other, with a champion of their own people, each with his own arms: the victory of the one or the other is looked upon as a precedent.

11. *The conduct of public business.*

The nobles make decisions about lesser matters, all freemen about things of greater significance, with this proviso, nonetheless, that those subjects of which ultimate judgment is in the hands of the mass of people receive preliminary consideration among the nobles. They hold meetings on specified days, unless something has occurred unexpectedly and suddenly, either at the new or full moon; they consider this the most auspicious beginning for carrying on business. Nor do they count the number

---

[4] These have just been mentioned at the end of chapter 9.

Ethnographical monograph, but also an "Utopia". It is a very subtle polemic here (pag. 73)

of days, as we do, but the number of nights. So they fix and settle their appointments: the night seems to lead on the day. The following is a fault that springs from their liberty, the fact that they do not assemble at the same time nor as if under orders, but two or three days are wasted by the delay of those who are coming together. When the crowd thinks it opportune, they sit down fully armed. Silence is demanded by the priests, who then also have the right of compulsion. Soon the king or the chieftains are heard, in accordance with the age, nobility, glory in war, and eloquence of each, with the influence of persuasion being greater than the power to command. If a proposal has displeased them, they show their displeasure with a roar; but if it has won favor; they bang their *frameae* together: the most prestigious kind of approval is praise with arms.

12. *Punishment of crime; the various penalties.*

It is also permitted to make an accusation before the council and to bring a capital charge. There is a variety of penalties in accordance with the crime: traitors and deserters they hang from trees, cowards and the unwarlike and those who have perverted their persons they plunge in the mire of a swamp, with a basket put over them.[5] The distinction in punishment shows their belief that violent crimes should be displayed while they are being punished, but disgraceful acts should be concealed. But there is punishment also for less significant wrongdoings in accordance with equity: those convicted are fined a number of horses or cattle. Part of the fine is paid to the king or the state, part to the individual who is being compensated or to his relatives. Chieftains who pronounce justice throughout the cantons and villages are also selected in the same councils; each has one hundred associates from the people who serve as an advisory council and as a source of authority.

13. *Bearing arms is the mark of maturity. The importance of the retinue.*

To continue, then, they carry on no business of a public or private nature except in arms. But it is not the custom for anyone to assume arms before the community has obtained evidence that he will be worthy of them. Then, in the council itself, either one

[5] The reason for the wicker basket was either to prevent the ghost of the deceased from escaping or, perhaps more practicably, "to prevent the body from rising to the surface" (Anderson).

of the chieftains or the father or relatives present the young man with shield and *framea:* among the Germans these are the equivalent of the toga, this is the first honor of young manhood; before this, they seem part of the household, thereafter part of the state. Particularly eminent birth or the great achievements of their fathers win the rank of chieftain even for very young men; they attach themselves to other more mature men who have reputations of long standing, and it is not a matter of shame to be seen in their entourage. Nay, the entourage itself has ranks, in accordance with the judgment of him whom they are following; and thus there is great rivalry among a man's followers, who has the leading position with their chief, and among the chieftains, who has the largest number of followers and the fiercest. This constitutes their honor and strength, always to be surrounded by a great band of chosen young men; this is prestige in peace and protection in war. And each one has this renown and glory, not only in his own tribe but also among neighboring states, if he excels by reason of the size and bravery of his entourage; for the chieftains are sought out by embassies and honored with gifts and frequently bring wars to an end by their very reputation.

14. *Honor in battle; love of war and dislike of peace.*

When they have come into battle, it is shameful for the chieftain to be excelled in valor, shameful for the entourage not to match the valor of the chieftain. Furthermore, it is shocking and disgraceful for all of one's life to have survived one's chieftain and left the battle: the prime obligation of the entourage's allegiance is to protect and guard him and to credit their own brave deeds to his glory: the chieftains fight for victory, the entourage for the chieftain. If the state in which they were born should be drowsing in long peace and leisure, many noble young men of their own accord seek those tribes which are then waging some war, since quiet is displeasing to the race and they become famous more easily in the midst of dangers, and one would not maintain a large retinue except by violence and war. For they claim from the generosity of their chieftain that glorious war horse, that renowned *framea* which will be bloodied and victorious; for banquets and provisions, not luxurious yet abundant, serve as pay. The wherewithal for generosity is obtained through wars and plunder, nor would one as easily persuade them to plow the earth or await the yearly crop as to challenge the enemy and earn wounds; nay, on the contrary, it seems slothful and lazy to gain by sweat what one could win by blood.

15. *Their surprising devotion to inactivity.*

Whenever they are not involved in wars, they devote little time to hunting, much more to leisure, with attention focused on sleep and food, all the bravest and most warlike men doing nothing, with the care of the home and household and fields assigned to the women and the old men and the most feeble of the family: they themselves lounge around, by an extraordinary contradiction of nature, since the same men so love inactivity and hate peace. It is the custom for states to bring to the chieftains, voluntarily and by individual contribution, offerings of cattle and crops, which, accepted as a token of honor, even support their requirements. The chieftains gain particular satisfaction from the gifts of neighboring tribes, which are sent not only by individuals but on behalf of the entire people—choice horses, magnificent weapons, decorations and neck chains; now we have taught them even to accept money.

Chapters 16–27. Private life.

16. *The absence of cities; the German dwellings.*

It is common knowledge that the peoples of the Germans do not live in cities, and they do not even like their homes to be joined together. They live separated and scattered, as a spring or a field or a grove has attracted them. They do not plan their villages in our manner with buildings joined together and next to one another: each one has an open area around his home, whether as a protection against the disasters of fire or because of a lack of skill in building. They make no use at all of stones or tiles:[6] they use unshaped timber for everything without regard to appearance or aesthetic pleasure. Certain parts they coat with greater care with an earth so pure and gleaming that it looks like painting and colored drawings. They are also accustomed to dig underground chambers and they cover them with a great deal of dung; these serve as a retreat against winter and a storage area for crops, since places[7] of this kind lessen the bitterness of the cold and, if ever an enemy comes, he lays waste the open places while the hidden and buried ones are unknown or escape attention for the very reason that they have to be searched for.

17. *Clothing and the way it is worn.*

The clothing common to all consists of a cloak held together

---

[6] Not roof tiles, but wall tiles, namely, bricks that faced concrete.
[7] I prefer the reading *loci* to Önnerfors's *lacus*.

with a pin or, if there is none, a thorn: wearing no other clothing, they pass whole days next to the hearth and fire. The wealth-
iest men[8] are distinguished by a garment that is not flowing as
that of the Sarmatians and Parthians but tight and displaying
every limb. They also wear animal skins, those nearest the river-
banks with no concern for style, those farther inland with more
elegance, since they get no finery through trade. They select the
wild animals and decorate their hides with spots from the skins
of animals which the farther ocean and the unknown sea
produce. And the women have the same garb as the men except
that the women are more often dressed in linen clothes and em-
broider them with purple, and do not fashion part of the upper
garment into sleeves, but the whole arm is bare; and the adjacent part of the breast is also exposed.

18. *The sanctity of marriage and the relationship of husband and wife.*

In spite of this, marriages there are strict, and one would praise
no other aspect of their civilization more. For almost alone of the
barbarians they are content with one wife apiece with only a
very few exceptions, who are the objects of many offers of marriages not because of their own lust but on account of their high
rank. The wife does not bring a dowry to the husband, but
rather the reverse occurs. Parents and relatives are present and
pass judgment upon the gifts, gifts not suited to womanly pleasure nor with which the new bride may deck herself out, but
cattle and a bridled horse and a shield with *framea* and sword. In
return for these gifts a wife is obtained, and she in turn brings
the man some weapon: they consider this exchange of gifts their
greatest bond, these their sacred rites, these their marriage divinities. So that the woman may not think herself beyond the
contemplation of brave acts and unaffected by the disasters of
wars, she is reminded by the very first ceremonies with which
her marriage begins that she comes as a partner in labors and
dangers, who will suffer and dare the same thing as her husband in peace, the same thing in war: this the yoked oxen, this
the caparisoned horse, this the gift of arms declare. So must she
live and die, with the understanding that she is receiving things
she is to hand on to her children, unimpaired and in worthy
state, which her daughters-in-law may receive and which may
be handed on again to grandchildren.

[8]I interpret this to mean that *omnibus* at the beginning of the chapter includes
the *locupletissimi*, not that the great mass are contrasted with the wealthy men.
The cloak is common to all, only a few have another garment.

This books seems more appropriate to Augustus's moral revival

19. *The punishment for adultery.*

As a result, they live with chastity secured, corrupted by no attractions of games, by no seductions of banquets. Men and women are alike ignorant of secret correspondence. Although their population is so great, there are very few cases of adultery, the punishment for which is immediate and left to the husbands: in the presence of her relatives, the husband drives her naked from the home, with her hair cut off, and whips her through the whole village. Indeed, there is no pardon for prostituted chastity; such a woman would not find a husband regardless of her beauty, youth, or wealth. There no one laughs at vices, and corruption and being corrupted are not excused by invoking the "times." Indeed, those states are still better in which only virgins marry and the hope and prayer of a wife are accomplished once and for all. Thus they receive one husband as they have received one body and one life, that there may be no further thought on the matter, no continuing desire, that they may esteem not their husbands, so to speak, but the state of marriage. It is considered a crime to limit the number of children or to put to death any of the children born after the first, and there good customs have greater influence than good laws elsewhere.

20. *The upbringing of the young and their late marriages. Inheritance.*

In every home the young, naked and dirty, grow to possess these limbs, these bodies, which we admire. His own mother nurses each one, and the children are not handed over to servants or nursemaids. You would not distinguish master and slave by any niceties of upbringing: they live amidst the same animals and on the same ground until age sets the freeborn apart and valor recognizes them as her own. The young men experience love late, and for this reason their strength is not exhausted. Nor are the girls hurried into marriage; they have the same youthful vigor and similar stature: they are well matched in age and strength when they enter upon marriage, and the children reproduce the strength of their parents. The sons of sisters have as great honor with their uncle as with their father. Certain individuals think that this bond of blood is holier and closer and insist upon it more in receiving hostages, with the reasoning that they control the emotions more firmly and the family more widely. Nonetheless, each person's own children are his heirs and successors, and there is no will. If there are no children, the next priority in inheritance is held by brothers, paternal uncles, and maternal uncles. The more blood relatives

the reference to the dowry is clear

the reference to the Rome 7

and marriage relations there are, the more agreeable is one's old age; and there are no rewards for childlessness.

21. *Feuds and friendships continue. The Germans' generosity in hospitality.*

There is an obligation to undertake the personal feuds as well as the friendships of one's father or blood relative, but the feuds do not continue without possibility of settlement, for even murder is atoned for by a specific number of cattle and sheep and the entire family accepts the settlement, with advantage to the community, since feuds are the more dangerous when joined with freedom.

No other people indulge more freely in feasts and hospitality. It is considered a sin to drive any human being from one's house; each one offers a banquet as generous as his fortune permits. When this has run out, he who had just been the host becomes the guide and companion to more hospitality; they go to the next home though uninvited. Nor does that make any difference: they are received with comparable welcome. No one makes any distinction between a person known and unknown as far as the right of hospitality is involved. It is customary to give the guest whatever he has asked for on his departure; and there is the same frankness in asking for something in return. They delight in gifts, but neither attach any conditions to what they have given nor feel bound by what they have received.

22. *The daily routine; the importance of banquets.*

Immediately upon arising from sleep, which they generally extend into the day, they wash, mostly with warm water, as is to be expected among a people where winter rules a great part of the year. After washing they take food: each person has his individual seat and his own table. Then they proceed, under arms, to their tasks and, no less often, to banquets. It is not disgraceful for anyone to pass day and night in drinking. As is common among drunken men, frequent quarrels occur, which are rarely settled just by insults but more often by murder and wounds. Yet they generally take counsel in banquets about reconciling enemies with each other, about entering upon marriage relationships, and about choosing chieftains, finally about peace and war, with the belief that at no other time does the mind lie more open to honest thoughts or grow more enthusiastic for great ones. The race, without natural or acquired cunning, even reveals its innermost contemplations in spontaneous good humor; therefore every person's thought is laid bare and exposed. The matter is reconsidered on the following day, and they have due respect for both occasions: they deliberate while they know not how to act falsely, they decide while they are unable to make a mistake.

23. *Food and drink. The Germans' drunkenness.*

They have a beverage made from barley or wheat, fermented into something like wine;[9] those nearest the frontier also purchase wine. Their foods are simple, wild fruits, fresh game, or curdled milk: they satisfy their hunger without fancy preparation and without seasonings. They do not have the same moderation regarding thirst. If one would indulge their intoxication by furnishing as much drink as they long for, they will be conquered no less easily by their vices than by arms.

24. *Their chief entertainments.*

There is one and the same kind of entertainment in every gathering: young men, stripped, who practise the sport, leap among swords and *frameae* pointed at them. Practice has produced skill, skill in turn grace, but not for profit or reward: the pleasure of the spectators is the only reward for the sport, however bold it may be. While sober they play dice as one of their serious pursuits, which one would wonder at, with such great recklessness in winning or losing that, when all else has been exhausted, they put their liberty and persons up as the stake on the very last throw. The loser enters voluntary slavery: though he may be younger and stronger, he allows himself to be bound and sold. There is perverse stubbornness in this business: they themselves call it honor. They sell slaves of this category, so that the winners may also free themselves from the shame of their win.

25. *Slaves and freedmen.*

They do not make use of the other slaves as we do, with functions assigned throughout the household: each slave is master of his own residence and his own home. The master imposes an amount of grain or cattle or cloth upon him as upon a tenant farmer, and the slave's obedience extends to this point: the master's wife and children accomplish the remaining tasks of the

[9]Beer.

home. It is a rare thing to whip a slave and to punish him with chains and hard labor: they are accustomed to kill them, not for sternness of discipline, but in an outburst of anger, as with a personal enemy, except that when dealing with a slave there is no fear of punishment. The status of freedmen is only a little above that of slaves, rarely with any influence in the home and never any in the state, with the exception only of those tribes that are under the rule of kings. For there they rise even above freeborn men and above those of noble birth: among others, the inferiority of freedmen is a proof of liberty.

26. *Interest on money is unknown. Land distribution and agriculture.*

To put capital to work and to increase it by lending at interest is unknown; and for this reason they are protected against it more effectively than if it had been prohibited. Cultivable lands are occupied by all in common, proportionate to the number of cultivators, and they then divide these among themselves according to rank; the great extent of the fields renders the division easy. They change their ploughlands year by year, and there is land left over. For, with land so fertile and abundant, they do not strive with their labor to plant orchards and set aside meadows and irrigate gardens: corn is the only crop required of the earth. As a result they do not even divide the year itself into as many seasons as we do: winter and spring and summer are known and have names, the name and products alike of autumn are unknown.

27. *Burials and funerals.*

There is no pomp in their funerals: their only observance is that the bodies of famous men are cremated with specific kinds of wood. They do not heap the pile of the pyre with clothing and perfumes: the deceased's weapons are put on the fire, as well as his horse in the case of certain individuals. A raised mound of earth serves as the tomb: they disdain the lofty and extravagant distinction of monuments because they are heavy upon the dead. They quickly put aside their lamentations and tears, their grief and sadness slowly. It is honorable for women to grieve, for men to remember.

This much we have learned in general concerning the origin and customs of all the Germans; now I shall explain how much the institutions and practices of individual tribes differ from each other and what peoples have migrated from Germany into the Gallic provinces.

Chapters 28–37. The tribes of the west and northwest, following the line of the Rhine from south to north.

28. *The difficulty of distinguishing Germans from Gauls and other peoples.*

The Deified Julius, the most authoritative of writers, reports[10] that the power of the Gauls was greater in times past; and for this reason one can believe that the Gauls even migrated into Germany. For how small an obstacle was a river to keep each tribe, whenever it had become powerful, from seizing and changing sites that were still common and not divided among powerful kingdoms? Thus the Helvetii occupied the area between the Hercynian Forest and the rivers Rhine and Main, and the Boii the territory beyond; both are Gallic tribes. There still remains the name of Bohemia and it records the ancient tradition of the place although the inhabitants are different. But whether the Aravisci crossed from the Osi, a Germanic people, into Pannonia, or the Osi into Germany from the Aravisci,[11] since they still use the same language, institutions, and customs, is impossible to determine, because the advantages and disadvantages of both banks of the river were the same, when in time past there were the same poverty and the same liberty. The Treveri and Nervii are especially desirous of claiming Germanic origin, as if by this glory of blood they would be freed from resemblance to the unwarlike indolence of the Gauls. Peoples who are unquestionably German occupy the very bank of the Rhine, the Vangiones, Triboci, Nemetes. Not even the Ubii, although they have earned their status as a Roman colony and more willingly call themselves Agrippinenses from the name of their founder,[12] blush at their origin; they once crossed over and were settled above the very bank of the Rhine after their reliability had been put to the test, to keep others from crossing, not themselves to be kept under guard.

29. *The special status of the Batavians and the Mattiaci. The problem of the agri decumates.*

The Batavians, who of all these tribes excel in bravery, inhabit a

---

[10] Julius Caesar, in the *Gallic War* 6.24.

[11] In chapter 43, Tacitus clearly states that the Osi are not Germanic. Either the phrase *Germanorum natione* in the present chapter is a gloss or Tacitus is inconsistent in his statements.

[12] *Colonia Claudia Ara Agrippinensis,* the modern Cologne, was established in A.D. 50 by the emperor Claudius, who gave it the name of his wife, Agrippina.

small stretch on the bank, but chiefly an island of the Rhine river; they were once a people of the Chatti who moved to this region as a result of internal faction, where they were destined to become a part of the Roman Empire. The privilege that is a token of their ancient alliance remains; for they are not insulted by tributes nor does the tax collector wear them down: they are exempt from burdensome duties and from special contributions and, kept on the sidelines only for use in battle, just like weapons and armor, are reserved for wars. The tribe of the Mattiaci has the same allegiance toward us; for the greatness of the Roman people extended respect for the empire beyond the Rhine and, in consequence, beyond its ancient boundaries. Thus they live, in geographical terms, on their own side, in spirit and inclination they are with us, like the Batavians in other respects, except that, in addition, they have greater energy because of the very soil and climate of their land.

I would not reckon those who work the *agri decumates*[13] among the peoples of Germany, although they have settled beyond the Rhine and Danube: the most inconsequential of the Gauls, made bold by their want, have occupied land that was insecurely held; then, when a frontier road had been laid and garrisons had been stationed in forward positions, they were considered a corner of empire and part of the province.

30. *The Chatti, their territory and characteristics.*

Beyond these are the Chatti, whose territory begins at the Hercynian Forest, where the country is not as flat and swampy as that of the other states that Germany embraces in its extent, since the hills extend through their territory and only gradually become less frequent, and the Hercynian Forest accompanies its Chatti to its limits and sets them down. The tribe is distinguished by hardier bodies, sinewy limbs, a threatening countenance, and greater liveliness of mind. Inasmuch as they are Germans, they have considerable judgment and skill: they choose their commanders and obey them, know how to keep their ranks, recognize opportunities, delay their attacks, map out the day, entrench themselves at night, consider fortune doubtful but bravery sure, and, a thing that is a very rare trait and one not granted except to Roman discipline, they place more confidence

[13] The *agri decumates* were the area between the courses of the Rhine and Danube that was included within the frontier established by Domitian and incorporated in the province of Upper Germany. Today it would be roughly equivalent to the southwestern corner of Germany.

in the general than in the army. All their strength is in the infantry, whom they load down with tools and provisions in addition
to their arms: you would see others go off to battle; the Chatti,
however, go off to war. Sallies and a chance fight are rare occurrences. Indeed it is the particular assignment of a cavalry force to
win victory quickly and to withdraw quickly: speed is akin to
terror, deliberateness is closer to resolute courage.

31. Their unusual customs.

The following custom, rarely practiced by the other German
peoples and dependent upon the personal daring of each individual, is general among the Chatti, namely to let their hair and
beard grow long as soon as they have reached maturity and not
to cut off the face's garb, which is vowed and owed to bravery,
unless they have slain an enemy. They uncover their brows
while standing over his bloody, despoiled corpse and claim that
they have at last paid back the debt of their birth and have thus
shown themselves worthy of country and parents. That shaggy
filth remains for the cowardly and unwarlike. In addition, all the
bravest men wear an iron ring (which is a mark of disgrace for
the race) as a bond until they may release themselves from it
by the slaughter of an enemy. This fashion pleases very many of
the Chatti, and they grow old marked out in this way, conspicu-
ous both to the enemy and their own people. The beginning of
all battles rests with them; they are always the first line of battle
and furnish a startling view; for not even in peace do they relax
their terrifying appearance. No one has a home or field or any
occupation at all: they are given food by whatever person they
have come to visit, extravagant with another's property, scornful
of their own, until feeble old age renders them unequal to such
hardy bravery.

32. The Usipi and Tencteri.

Next to the Chatti,[14] the Usipi and Tencteri live along the Rhine,
which now has a definite channel and is thus adequate to serve
as a boundary. Besides the usual distinction in war, the Tencteri
excel in skill of horsemanship, and the infantry has no greater
prestige among the Chatti than the cavalry does for the Tencteri.
This their ancestors established, this the descendants copy.
These are the pastimes of children and the rivalry of young men:

---

[14]Tacitus is now discussing the tribes from south to north, following the
course of the Rhine.

the old men continue to practice them. Horses are bequeathed with the slaves and home and the rights of inheritance: a son is the recipient, yet not the oldest, as with the rest of the property, but the one who stands out by his ferocity and superiority in war.

33. *The extirpation of the Bructeri, as a favor to Rome from the gods.*

The Bructeri once lived next to the Tencteri; now it is reported that the Chamavi and Angrivarii entered their territory, drove out the Bructeri, and completely wiped them out, with the support of neighboring tribes, whether because of hatred of their haughtiness or the attraction of booty or a certain kindliness of the gods toward us; for they even provided us the spectacle of a battle. More than sixty thousand fell, not by the arms and weapons of the Romans, but, more magnificent still, to delight our eyes. Let there continue and endure, I pray, among foreign peoples, if not affection for us, at least hatred for one another, since, as the destiny of empire drives us on, fortune can furnish us nothing greater than the discord of the enemy.[15]

34. *Tribes farther north. Rome's experience with the ocean there.*

The Dulgubini and Chasuarii and other tribes even less worthy of record bound the Angrivarii and Chamavi on the east; the Frisii meet them in the west. The greater and lesser Frisii get their names on the basis of their respective power. Both tribes are bordered by the Rhine all the way to the ocean and have besides within their territory huge lakes that have been navigated even by Roman fleets. Nay, we have even tried the ocean itself there: and legend has reported that there still exist columns of Hercules, either because Hercules did come there or we have agreed to assign to his greatness whatever is anywhere remarkable. Nor did Drusus Germanicus lack daring, but the ocean blocked his exploration of itself as well as of the achievements of Hercules. Then no one made the attempt, and it seemed more pious and reverent to believe in the deeds of the gods than to understand them.

35. *The nobility and power of the Chauci.*

So much we know of Germany to the west; it continues to the north with a great sweep. And first off, the tribe of the Chauci,

---

[15] The tone of the phrase *urgentibus imperii fatis* has been much discussed. Perhaps the prevailing view is that Tacitus here displays his pessimism and fear about the future of the empire. Yet it may be countered that the year 98, marked

although it begins from the Frisii and occupies part of the coast, borders all the tribes I have mentioned, until it makes a bend all the way to the Chatti. Not only do the Chauci possess so great an extent of land but they also fill it; they are the noblest people among the Germans and of such character that they prefer to look out for their greatness with fair play. Without greed, without violent passion, quiet and off by themselves, they bring about no wars, lay no one waste by rapine or robbery. This is particular proof of their high character and strength, that they do not gain their superiority through aggression; nonetheless, all have their arms at hand and, if a situation demands it, there is an army, very powerful in men and horses; and they have the same renown when they are at peace.

36. *The once-powerful Cherusci have now become weak.*

On the flank of the Chauci and the Chatti, the Cherusci, since they have been unprovoked, have fostered an excessive and enervating peace for a long time; and this furnished greater satisfaction than safety, since it is foolish to be peaceable among violent and strong peoples: where might is the basis of action, moderation and honorable behavior are attributes of the more powerful. Thus the Cherusci, who were once "good and righteous," are now called lazy and stupid; good luck was considered wisdom for the victorious Chatti. And the Fosi, a neighboring tribe, were involved in the ruin of the Cherusci and shared equally in disaster, although they had been junior partners in prosperity.

37. *A sketch of Rome's dealings with the Germans over a period of more than two centuries, with domination not yet gained.*

Nearest the ocean, the Cimbri, a state now small but great in glory, occupy the same peninsula of Germany. And there remain widely scattered traces of their ancient renown, camps of great size on both sides of the Rhine, by the extent of which one may measure even now the power and numbers of the tribe and the credibility of so great a migration. Our city was in its 640th year when the arms of the Cimbri were first heard of, in the consulship of Caecilius Metellus and Papirius Carbo. If we should count from that year to the second consulship of the Emperor Trajan, the sum is about 210 years: for so long a time has the

---

by the accession of Trajan as emperor, seems hardly the time for despondency and gloom. I have tried to convey an optimistic rather than a pessimistic note.

conquest of Germany been in progress.[16] In the course of so extended a period there have been many disasters on both sides. Not the Samnites, not the Carthaginians, not Spain or Gaul, not even the Parthians have more often given us warning: for the liberty of the Germans is a greater threat than the kingdom of Arsaces.[17] For with what else could the East mock us except the death of Crassus, and it itself was crushed under Ventidius with the loss of Pacorus?[18] But the Germans robbed the Roman people of five consular armies one after another, with Carbo and Cassius and Aurelius Scaurus and Servilius Caepio and Mallius Maximus routed or captured, and even stripped Augustus of Varus and his three legions; and not without loss did Gaius Marius defeat them in Italy, the Deified Julius in Gaul, Drusus and Nero and Germanicus in their own territories; soon the great threats of Gaius Caesar were turned to mockery.[19] Then there was peace, until, when opportunity had been offered by our internal strife and civil wars, they stormed the winter quarters of legions and even aimed at the Gallic provinces;[20] and when they had again been beaten, thereafter, in recent times, they appeared in triumphal processions rather than being actually conquered.

Chapters 38–43. The Suebic tribes of the east and north, following the line of the Danube from west to east.

38. The Suebi and their chief characteristics.

Now we must speak about the Suebi, of whom there is no single nation, as there is of the Chatti or Tencteri; for they possess the greater part of Germany and are besides divided into separate tribes with individual names, although they are called Suebi generically. It is a characteristic of the people to pull their hair back and to tie it in a knot: this is how the Suebi are distinguished from the rest of the Germans and their freeborn from their slaves.

[16]The canonical date for the foundation of Rome, as determined by Varro in the first century B.C., was April 21, 753 B.C. The consulship of Metellus and Carbo was in 113; thus Tacitus' dating is precise, for the news of the invasion came in early spring. Trajan's second consulship was in A.D. 98.

[17]The kings of Parthia traditionally took the name Arsaces as a title.

[18]Crassus died in 53 B.C.; Ventidius was victorious over the Parthians in 38 B.C.; Pacorus was the son of the king of Parthia.

[19]The five consular armies were lost between 113–105 B.C.; Varus' disaster was A.D. 9. The other references are to Marius, 101 B.C.; Caesar, 58–55 B.C.; Drusus, 12–9 B.C.; Nero, the later emperor Tiberius, nine campaigns between 9 B.C. and A.D. 11; Germanicus, A.D. 14–16; Gaius Caesar, the emperor Caligula, A.D. 39.

[20]The revolt of Civilis began in A.D. 69, the year of the four emperors, and was crushed in the following year.

This characteristic is occasionally found among other tribes, whether stemming from some relationship with the Suebi or, which often happens, from imitation, and only within the period of youth; among the Suebi it remains until they are gray-headed; they pull their bristling hair back and often tie it on the very top of the head; the chieftains have it even more intricately arranged. Herein is their care for their personal appearance, but it is harmless, for they do not do it to love or to be loved, but they adorn themselves for the eyes of the enemy when they go to war, with their hair arranged to increase their height and thus strike terror.

39. *The Semnones and their religious practice.*

Tradition has it that the Semnones are the most ancient and noble of the Suebi; credibility in their antiquity is confirmed by a religious practice. At an appointed time, all the peoples of the same blood, represented by embassies, come together into a forest hallowed by the auguries of their ancestors and by ancient awe and, with the slaying of a human being in public sacrifice, they celebrate the dread beginnings of barbarian ritual. There is another display of reverence for the grove: no one enters it unless he has been bound by a cord, as a token of his inferiority and a display of the divinity's power. If he has by chance stumbled, it is not permitted for him to raise himself and get up: he rolls forward on the ground. And the whole superstition rests upon the view that from there spring the tribe's origins, there dwells the god who rules over all, to whom all else is subordinate and inferior. The prosperity of the Semnones also lends them prestige: they live in a hundred cantons, and because of their great number they consider themselves the chief of the Suebi.

40. *The Langobardi and other tribes. The worship of the goddess Nerthus.*

On the other hand, their small number gives the Langobardi renown: though surrounded by very many and very powerful tribes, they are safe not through submission but by taking risks in battle. Next to them, the Reudigni, Aviones, Anglii, Varini, Eudoses, Suarines, and Nuitones are protected by rivers or by forests. Nor is there anything remarkable in the individual tribes, save that they worship Nerthus, that is, Mother Earth, in common and think that she participates in the affairs of men and is carried in procession among the peoples. On an island of the ocean there is a sacred grove, and in it a consecrated wagon, covered by a cloth; only the priest is permitted to touch it. He perceives that the goddess is present in the shrine and follows her with great reverence as she is drawn along by cows. Then days are joyous, and whichever places she deems worthy of her visit as a guest are festive. They do not enter upon wars, they do not take up arms; all iron is locked up; only at this time are peace and quiet known and only at this time loved, until the same priest restores the goddess to her holy place when she has had enough association with mortals. Soon the carriage and the garments and, if you should wish to believe it, the divinity herself are bathed in an isolated lake. Slaves assist, whom the lake at once swallows up. From this stems the mystic dread and the holy ignorance of what that divinity is which they see only on the verge of death.

41. *The special position of the Hermunduri.*

And indeed this part of the Suebi extends to the more remote areas of Germany: the state of the Hermunduri, which is faithful to the Romans, is nearer to us, to follow the course of the Danube now as a little before I followed that of the Rhine;[21] for this reason they are the only ones of the Germans who have commercial relations not merely on the riverbank, but well inside the frontier and even in the very magnificent colony of the province of Raetia.[22] They cross over everywhere and without control; and, while we display to other tribes only our arms and camps, to these we have opened up our homes and villas since they do not covet them. The Elbe rises in the territory of the Hermunduri; a river that was once famous and known, now it is only a name.

42. *The Marcomani and the Quadi are supported by the Romans.*

Next to the Hermunduri dwell the Naristi and then the Marcomani and Quadi. The prestige and strength of the Marcomani are especially high, and their very home was won by bravery, when they drove out the Boii long ago. Nor do the Naristi or Quadi fall short of them. And these tribes are, so to speak, the frontier of Germany, as far as it is bordered by the Danube. Up to our own day the Marcomani and Quadi have had kings chosen

---

[21] See note 14. Tacitus now follows the Danube from west to east.
[22] *Augusta Vindelicum*, the modern Augsburg.

from their own race, the noble stock of Maroboduus and Tudrus; now they also put up with foreigners, but the kings' coercive and personal authority rests upon Roman backing. They are rarely supported by our arms, more frequently by money, and they are no less powerful for that.

43. *Eastern Suebic tribes and the special features of some.*

On the north, the Marsigni, Cotini, Osi, and Buri border the rear of the Marcomani and Quadi. Of these, the Marsigni and Buri are like the Suebi in language and way of life; a Gallic language argues strongly that the Cotini are not Germans, as does a Pannonian language for the Osi, as well as the fact that they tolerate tributes. The Sarmatians impose part of the tribute upon them as being of foreign birth, the Quadi impose the rest; the Cotini, to make their shame greater, even mine iron. All these peoples have settled upon a few stretches of level country, but mainly groves and the heights of mountains. For a continuous ridge of mountains divides and bisects Suebia, beyond which live very many tribes; of these the nation of the Lugii, spread over many states, has the widest extent. It will be sufficient to name the strongest: Harii, Helvecones, Manimi, Helysii, Nahanarvali. Among the Nahanarvali there is shown a grove of an ancient rite. A priest in woman's attire officiates, but people relate that the gods are equivalent to the Roman Castor and Pollux. That is the character of the divinity, the name is Alci. There are no images, no trace of foreign belief; nevertheless, they worship them as brothers, as young men. But to continue, the Harii, besides their strength, in which they excel the peoples mentioned a little above, are a fierce people who enhance their natural savageness by art and the choice of time. Their shields are black, their bodies are painted black; they choose black nights for battles and produce terror by the mere appearance, terrifying and shadowy, of a ghostly army. No enemy can withstand a vision that is strange and, so to speak, diabolical; for in all battles the eyes are overcome first.

Chapters 44–46. The almost fairy-tale lands of the north.

44. *The Suiones and their culture.*

Beyond the Lugii are the Gotones, who are ruled by kings, a little more strictly than the other tribes of the Germans, but not yet, nonetheless, to the point of suppression of liberty. Then, right along the ocean are the Rugii and Lemovii; characteristic of all these tribes are round shields, short swords, and obedience to their kings.

Next, the states of the Suiones, in the ocean itself, are powerful in fleets as well as men and arms. The shape of their ships is different in this, that a prow at each end presents a front always ready for landing. They neither guide them with sails nor attach oars to the sides in regular order: the oars are loose, as is the case on certain rivers, and the rowing can be changed from one direction to the other, as circumstance requires. Wealth also has honor among them, and one man rules on this basis, here with no restrictions, with no uncertain right to obedience. Nor does every man keep his weapons, as among the rest of the Germans, but they are kept locked up under guard, and the guard is a slave, since the ocean prevents sudden attacks of the enemy, and further the idle hands of armed men easily follow their fancy: for it is to the king's advantage to put neither a noble nor a freeborn man nor even a freedman in charge of the arms.

45. *The sea to the extreme north. The tribe of the Aestii and their civilization.*

Beyond the Suiones is another sea, sluggish and almost unmoved; there is belief that the earth is surrounded and enclosed by it for this reason, because the last glow of the already setting sun lasts till the dawn so brightly that it dims the stars; further, there is added the popular conviction that the sound of the rising sun is heard and the shapes of the sun's horses and the rays of his head are seen. Only so far does the world extend—and the report of it is true. Now then, the tribes of the Aestii, who have the customs and appearance of the Suebi, a language closer to the British, are located on the right shore of the Suebic sea. They worship the mother of the gods. They wear amulets in the shape of boars as a mark of their belief: it renders the worshipper of the goddess safe even among enemies, in place of weapons and as a protection against all things. There is rare use of iron, frequent use of clubs. They cultivate grains and other crops of the earth with greater perseverance than expected, given the customary laziness of the Germans. But they also search out the sea, and they are the only ones to gather amber, which they call *glesum*, amidst the shoals and on the shore itself. Nor has it been investigated or ascertained what its nature is or what process produces it, since they are barbarians; nay even, for a long time it lay neglected among other things cast up by the sea, until our luxury gave it reputation. They have no use for it themselves: it is gathered in natural form, is transported shapeless, and they are amazed that they receive a price. Nevertheless, you would think that it was the sap of trees, since certain crawling and even winged animals are often visible in it, which, stuck in the liquid, are then held fast as the material hardens. I should therefore believe that, just as in distant parts of the East where incense and balsam are exuded, so there are unusually rich groves and woods in islands and lands of the West; the substances of these, drawn forth by the rays of the nearby sun and in liquid form, flow into the nearest sea and are washed up onto opposing shores by the force of storms. If you should test the nature of amber by bringing fire to it, it lights like a torch and produces a rich and smelly flame; soon it becomes viscous like pitch or resin.

The tribes of the Sithones join onto the Suiones. Like the latter in other respects, they are different in one thing, namely, that a woman rules: so much have they declined not only from freedom but also from slavery.

46. *Tribes beyond civilization to the north and east, with reports like fairy tales.*

This is the furthest extent of Suebia. I am uncertain whether I should assign the tribes of the Peucini and Venethi and Fenni to the Germans or the Sarmatians. And yet the Peucini, whom certain sources call the Bastarnae, are just like the Germans in language, manner of life, and in their fixed dwellings. Filthiness is common to all and slothfulness to their leading men. By mixed marriages they are getting to look like the Sarmatians in their coarse appearance. The Venethi have drawn much from the character of the Sarmatians; for in their plundering forays they wander through the whole stretch of forests and mountains that rise between the Peucini and the Fenni. These people, nevertheless, are rather to be recorded among the Germans, since they establish fixed homes and carry shields and get pleasure from traveling on foot and with speed: all these things are different from the practice of the Sarmatians, who live in the wagon and on horseback. The Fenni have astonishing savagery and squalid poverty: there are no arms, no horses, no household; herbs serve as their food, hides as their clothing, the ground as their bed; their only hopes are in their arrows, which they point with bones in the absence of iron. And the same hunt feeds men and women alike; for the latter accompany the men everywhere and claim their part in catching the spoil. The children have no other protection against wild animals and rains than being placed under some intertwined branches:[23] to this hut the young men return, this is their refuge when they are old. But they think it a happier state than to groan over the working of fields, to struggle at home-building, to deal with their own fortunes and those of others with hope and fear: without concern in their relations with men as well as with gods, they have attained a most difficult thing, not to have the need even to express a wish. The rest is now in the realm of fable, that the Hellusii and Oxiones have the faces and visages of men, the bodies and limbs of wild beasts: I shall leave this in abeyance as unproven.

[23] This refers to huts made of boughs and twigs.

Dialogue on Orators

Dialogue was a very popular literary form in antiquity. Plato is the best-known exponent of the genre; among the Romans, Cicero is the outstanding representative, in works such as *De re-publica*. The classic definition of the form stems from Diogenes Laertius, who probably lived in the third century A.D. He states that a dialogue is "a discourse consisting of question and answer on some philosophical or political subject, with due regard to the characters of the persons introduced and the choice of diction" (*Lives of the Philosophers* 3.48).

The theme of the *Dialogue on Orators* is clearly presented in the very first sentence. The question is raised why oratory is now so much inferior to what it used to be. Tacitus uses the Ciceronian form of the dialogue to report artistically a discussion on this subject which he had heard when he was a young man. The participants are four of the most renowned speakers of the day, all of whom, with the exception of Messalla, are provincial in origin, exemplifying the great influence that men from the provinces possessed, an evolution that culminated in the accession of the first non-Italian emperor, Trajan, barely twenty years after the dramatic date of this dialogue.

The scene is set at Curiatius Maternus' home; Marcus Aper and Julius Secundus call upon him the day after he had offended the feelings of very powerful men by the recitation of a play with views rather too liberal for the times. The first four chapters serve as introduction; Maternus states that he will give up his career as a pleader and devote himself exclusively to poetry. Aper, an enthusiastic and violent advocate of the new and modern style of oratory, argues fiercely, in chapters 5 through 10, that oratory is a more noble and useful occupation than poetry. Maternus rebuts him gently in chapters 11 through 13.

At this point, Vipstanus Messalla, the bearer of a great name of republican renown, enters and is apprised of the subject of discussion by Secundus. After stating that he had already devoted much thought to the subject, Messalla is asked to present his views. Messalla worships the achievements of the ancient orators; these feelings are assaulted by Aper in a long tirade covering chapters 15 through 23. Aper first sophistically argues that the word "ancient" should not be applied to Cicero and his contemporaries, who lived but yesterday, as it were, and then severely criticizes all the orators of the republic for various and sundry serious failings. Messalla, in chapters 25 to 27 (24 serves as a bridge), defends them in toto against the claims of the "moderns." But he is then reminded by Maternus that he has not yet explained why oratory now falls below the level it achieved a century and more ago.

The main part of the work now begins. Messalla argues that the responsibility rests with the current modes of training and education of children. Contrary to the strict and practical training prevalent in days gone by, children are now raised by nurses and slaves and are then sent to the schools of the rhetoricians, where they learn to speak prettily but to no purpose. They gain no experience in life.

Messalla is still speaking in chapter 35 when the text is broken by a lacuna. When the text begins anew, the speaker appears to be Maternus (more about this below), who continues to hold forth until the end of the dialogue, when the visitors depart in good humor. Maternus pinpoints the cause of oratory's decline in the changed political climate of the principate. In the chaos and anarchy of the last days of the republic, great policies of government were championed and thwarted by oratorical skill. But now, in the quiet days of the empire, all major decisions are made by the emperor, who is recognized as the single wisest person, *sapientissimus et unus*. With the absence of great issues, oratory has flagged, but one should not mourn its decline, for the state is now lawfully ordered. One may detect a sigh for the changed order in Maternus' remarks, but there is no question of his acceptance of the good that the imperial form of government had produced.

More scholarly discussion has centered upon the question of the lacuna than any other aspect of the work. Several points must be considered. In the view presented in the preceding paragraph, Secundus is left without any major role in the entire dialogue; indeed, he does nothing more than bring Messalla up to date when the latter appears. To many, this seems incomprehensible; they therefore assign him chapters 36 to 40 (as far as the words *Non de otiosa*), postulate another lacuna before these words, and claim that this second gap contains the end of Secundus' speech and the beginning of Maternus'. The objection that there is no evidence in the manuscripts for a second lacuna seems to me fatal to this reconstruction; lacunae do not customarily begin neatly at the end of a sentence and end at the beginning of another. Since it is impossible to estimate how many pages of the manuscripts have been lost, scholars have argued for a long lacuna and hence a speech for Secundus, with or without another gap in chapter 40, and for a short lacuna and hence no possibility for a speech for Secundus. I agree with the latter, and the results of this view are presented above.

With the *Dialogue on Orators*, Tacitus bids farewell to the field that had brought him his first literary fame, and he moves totally into history, in which the three short works had given him his apprenticeship. Had his great historical achievements come earlier than Quintilian's judgments on historians in Book 10 of his *Institutio oratoria*, Tacitus would unquestionably have supplanted Sallust as rival to Thucydides. What comments Quintilian would have made, we can perhaps surmise.

Dialogue on Orators

Chapters 1–4. Introduction. Maternus will devote himself to poetry.

1. *Tacitus will reproduce a discussion which he heard in his youth to answer the question why oratory is now inferior to what it was.*

You often ask me, Fabius Justus, why our age above all, barren and stripped of the glory of eloquence, scarcely retains the very name of "orator," although earlier periods bloomed with the renowned talents of so many distinguished orators. We do not even call any but the men of old "orators," while the skilled speakers of the present day are said to be pleaders and advocates and counselors, or anything you wish rather than orators. I should certainly scarcely dare to reply to your inquiry and undertake the burden of so significant a problem, a problem of such import that one must think ill of our abilities if we cannot attain the same standard, or of our taste if we are unwilling to attain it, had I to offer my own opinion. But I need only reproduce the conversation of men who were very eloquent, considering the times in which we live, whom I heard discussing this very question when I was still a young man. And so I do not need talent but the power of memory and recollection to present what I heard, subtly thought out and spoken with conviction, from men of great distinction, when each one offered different yet plausible reasons and displayed the unique quality of his feeling and understanding, and I shall retain the same categories and arguments and order of discussion. For there was even someone who took the opposite side and preferred the eloquence of our day to that of antiquity, with much abuse of, and scorn against, the latter.

2. *Two distinguished orators call upon Curiatius Maternus.*

Curiatius Maternus had given a public reading of his historical drama entitled *Cato;*[1] it was said that he had offended the feelings of powerful men, because (so ran the charge) he had forgot-

---

[1] From the moment of his suicide in 46 B.C. Cato, known as Uticensis from the city where he died, became a symbol of the republic crushed by the power of one man, Caesar. See Lucan's famous line: Victrix causa deis placuit, sed victa

ten himself in the plot of his play and had presented the views of Cato alone, and there was much talk in Rome about this. The next day Marcus Aper and Julius Secundus, who were the most renowned talents of the law courts at the time, called upon him. I not only used to listen to both of them with attention in the courts, but attended upon them in private and in public because of my passionate desire for these studies and a certain youthful enthusiasm, to drink in their conversations, discussions, and private rehearsals. Yet many thought, with malice, that Secundus lacked ready speech and that Aper had attained his reputation for eloquence rather by his natural talent and power than through literary training. On the contrary, Secundus had a style pure in diction, concise, and fluent enough, and Aper, who had been trained in every field, scorned, rather than was ignorant of, the study of literature, as if he would obtain greater glory for effort and enterprise if his talent seemed not to rely upon any supports of other fields of study.

3. *Maternus' tragedy* Cato *has given political offense. Aper chides him for his neglect of oratory.*

When we entered Maternus' room, then, we came upon him seated, with that play, which he had read on the previous day, in his hands. Then Secundus said: "Do not the comments of malicious people frighten you at all, so that you love the faults of your *Cato* a little less? Or have you taken it in hand to revise it with greater care and, by removing the parts that have given rise to misinterpretation, to make public a *Cato* who is not indeed better but nonetheless not so likely to cause trouble?"

Maternus responded: "You will read what Maternus considered his duty and you will recognize what you have heard. If *Cato* left anything unsaid, *Thyestes* will say it at the next reading; for I have already arranged the material for this play and have molded it in my mind. And I am eager to expedite the publication of this book so that I can devote myself totally to a new enterprise after finishing with this earlier one."

"Those tragedies of yours do not give you enough satisfaction," said Aper, "to keep you from spending all your time, at one time on *Medea* and at another indeed on *Thyestes*, to the complete neglect of your speeches and lawsuits, when the cases of so many friends and the client relationships of so many com-

---

Catoni. (The gods favored the winning side, but Cato the losers), *The Civil War* 1.128.

munities and towns summon you into the forum; you would scarcely have sufficient time for them even if you had not put this additional task upon yourself, to add Roman names such as Domitius and Cato and also events of our history to the tales of the Greeks."

4. *Maternus pleads the superiority of poetry.*

Then Maternus responded: "I should be upset by this sternness of yours if this continuing and constant disagreement had not almost become a habit with us. For you do not stop your abuse and attacks against poets, and I, whom you charge with neglect of my professional duties, everyday undertake this defense of poetry against you. I am therefore all the happier that a judge has been offered us, who will either forbid me to write poetry in the future or, and I have long been hoping for this, will also by his own prestige urge me to have no more to do with the difficulties of legal cases, in which I have labored more than enough, and to devote myself to that loftier and holier form of eloquence."

Chapters 5–10. Aper's rebuttal: oratory is nobler and more useful.

5. *Oratory is more useful than poetry.*

Secundus then replied: "Before Aper challenges me as a judge, I shall do what honorable and upright judges customarily do, namely, disqualify themselves in those cases in which it is clear that they have a prejudice for one of the parties. For certainly everyone knows that no one is closer to me in continuous friendship and personal relations than Saleius Bassus,[2] who is not only an excellent man but also a consummate poet. Furthermore, if poetry is put into the dock, I see no other defendant more richly endowed."

"I don't want Bassus to be worried," said Aper, "nor anyone else who cultivates the pursuit of poetry and literary renown, since they are unable to plead cases. For it is my intention, since we have found a judge for this dispute, not to allow Maternus to be defended by joining others to his case, but to charge him alone of all, because he, though gifted by nature for the vigorous eloquence of oratory, whereby he could simultaneously produce and preserve friendships, acquire connections, and become the patron of provinces, ignores the discipline that is beyond com-

---

[2]Bassus was an epic poet whose talent was praised by Quintilian (10. 1. 90).

pare in our state in terms of practical advantage; above all, it contributes to personal distinction and renown in the city and recognition in the entire empire and among all peoples. For if all our enterprises and actions should be directed to the utility of life, what is a source of greater security than to practice that skill whose possession, always at hand, enables you to protect your friends, assist strangers, and bring safety to those in danger and, as a bonus, produce fear and dread in those who are envious of you and are hostile to you, while all the time you are yourself free from danger and are guarded by a kind of continual power and authority, so to speak? The beneficent power of this ability is recognized in the secure protection afforded others when one's own affairs are prospering; but if one's own danger is threatened, indeed a breastplate and sword are not sturdier defense in battle than eloquence is to a defendant in danger, since it is at the same time a defensive and offensive weapon, with which you could equally well parry or attack either in a case pleaded before the people or before the senate or before the emperor. What other protection than his own eloquence did Eprius Marcellus recently have against the senators who were hostile to him? Well equipped and therefore threatening, he escaped Helvidius Priscus,[3] who, though eloquent and wise, was a novice and totally unskilled in contests of this kind. But I refrain from saying more about the utility of oratory, since I think that Maternus will least of all refute this part of my argument.

6. *Oratory furnishes pleasure and prestige.*

"I pass now to the pleasure produced by oratorical eloquence, the charm of which affects not some single moment but almost every day and indeed almost every hour. For what is a greater source of satisfaction for a spirit free, noble, and naturally inclined to honorable pleasures than to see his home always full and crowded with the gatherings of very distinguished men? And to know that this mark of honor is due not to his wealth or childless state or holding of some public office, but to himself? Do not men, on the contrary, who are childless, rich, powerful, often come to a man who is young and poor, to entrust to him their own cases or those of their friends? Is there any pleasure in great wealth and great power as real as to see that men who are

---

[3]Eprius Marcellus, a vicious informer under Nero, was three times prosecuted by Helvidius, each time without success. He committed suicide in 79. For Helvidius, see *Agricola* 2 and *Hist.* 4. 5.

members of ancient families and aged and who have influence throughout the world confess, in the midst of the greatest abundance of everything, that they do not have that which is the best thing? Now indeed what an escort and company of citizens there is, clad in their togas! What public prestige! What honor in the law courts! What of that pleasure of rising and standing among people who are silent and turn their attention to one man! To have the people come together and crowd close around and accept as their own whatever emotion the orator has displayed! I mention the outward joys of public speakers which are obvious even to the eyes of the ignorant; those which are internal and known only to orators are greater. If he produces a speech carefully worked out and rehearsed, there is a certain gravity and lasting quality not only in his manner of speaking but in his satisfaction; if he presents a novel and fresh oration not without some nervousness, his very lack of confidence adorns the outcome and produces greater pleasure. But there is particular pleasure in boldness and rashness that are extempore, for the products of genius, as of the earth, give greater pleasure when they spring up of their own accord, though others are sown and worked over for a long time.

7. *Aper's own successful career stems from his oratorical ability.*

"Indeed, to speak about myself, I did not find more enjoyable that day on which the senatorial stripe was presented to me or those on which I, a new man[4] and born in a city hardly favorable for a public career,[5] received the quaestorship or the tribunate or the praetorship, than I do those on which it is granted me, modest as this skill of mine in speaking may be, either to defend a client with success or to plead some case with good fortune before the court of one hundred[6] or to protect and defend the influential freedmen and procurators of the emperors before the emperor. Then I seem to myself to rise above the offices of tribune and praetor and consul, then I seem to possess something which, if it does not spring from our spirit, is not granted by imperial order nor comes with influence. Tell me now. What profession is there that should be compared in reputation and dis-

[4] A "new man" (*novus homo*) was the first member of a family to reach the consulate.

[5] Aper was born in Gaul, in a community that had little influence on the Roman political scene.

[6] The court of the *centumviri* at this time consisted of 180 members, although its original name was retained. It heard cases involving such matters as inheritance and wardship.

tinction with the glory of orators? Are orators not renowned in the city not only among men of business and affairs, but even among the young and inexperienced, who possess only good characters and high expectations of themselves? Whose names do parents din into their children's ears before theirs? Whom do even the ignorant and these common people call by name and point out with their fingers more often as they pass by? Even strangers and foreigners, as soon as they have come to Rome, seek out those men of whom they have already heard in their towns and colonies and yearn to recognize them, as it were.[7]

8. *Eprius Marcellus and Vibius Crispus have attained enormous wealth and influence through their power as speakers.*

"I should venture to claim that this Eprius Marcellus, about whom I just spoke, and Vibius Crispus (I prefer to use examples which are new and current rather than those distant and almost forgotten) are as well known in the farthest corners of the earth as in Capua or Vercellae, where they are said to have been born.[8] And this is not due to their wealth, though one of them has 200 million sesterces and the other 300 million[9] and it can be said that they gained that very wealth by virtue of their eloquence; their renown is rather due to oratorical ability, the divine nature and heavenly power of which have produced many examples, to be sure, in all ages, of the heights to which men have come by the power of genius; but these are examples, as I said before, which are very near and need not be learned of by hearsay but rather can be seen by our eyes. For, the lower and humbler their birth, the more abject their poverty, and the more pronounced the absence of all material advantages, all the more distinguished and illustrious proofs are they of the advantage of oratorical elo-quence, because, without the favor of birth and without for-tunes, neither gifted with a good character and one of them even unattractive in appearance, they have now for many years been the most powerful men of the state and were, as long as

[7] For a charming instance of this, see letter 9. 23 of Pliny the Younger.

[8] Vibius Crispus, another notorious informer, died at the age of 80 around the year 92. He was born in Vercellae, a town in Cisalpine Gaul; Capua was the lead-ing city of southern Italy.

[9] A sesterce is most easily reckoned as equivalent to a nickel, so that the for-tunes mentioned here would be about ten and fifteen million dollars. In real money values, however, the sums would have been much higher. These were fantastic fortunes; the greatest wealth recorded for any Roman of private status was four hundred million sesterces (twenty million dollars).

they wanted to be, the leading advocates of the forum. Now they are foremost in the friendship of the emperor and have all honor and are esteemed by the emperor himself with a certain kind of reverence, since Vespasian, an old man deserving of veneration who above all cares for the truth, knows full well that the rest of his friends indeed rely upon what they have received from him, things which it is easy for him to heap up and confer upon others, while Marcellus and Crispus brought to their friendship with him that which they had not received from the emperor and which could not be received from him. Among so many and such great advantages, images of famous people and laudatory inscriptions and statues hold the least important place, all of which, nonetheless, are by no means disdained, any more than wealth and riches; it is easier to find a person who scorns them than one who rejects them. Therefore we see that the homes of these men, who have devoted themselves to cases in the forum and the study of oratory since early manhood, have been loaded down with honors and decorations and wealth.

9. *Poetry furnishes brief pleasure and little tangible reward.*

"Poetry and versification, on the other hand, to which Maternus wishes to devote his entire life (for that was the point of departure from which the whole discussion flowed) do not win any honor for their authors nor do they produce any tangible benefits; on the contrary, they result in pleasure that is of brief duration and praise that is empty and unprofitable. Although your ears may rebel at these comments and what I am going to say next, Maternus, who gets any benefit if Agamemnon or Jason speaks with skill in your plays? Who for this reason goes home obligated to you because of a successful defense? Who escorts our Saleius, a distinguished poet or, to put it in more complimentary terms, a most eminent bard, to the forum or calls upon him or accompanies him home? Surely if a friend of his or a relative or, finally, he himself has fallen into some trouble, he will run to Secundus here or to you, Maternus, not because you are a poet or for you to make verses in his behalf; for Bassus has plenty of these at home, and though they are beautiful and charming, yet their fate is as follows: when he has hammered out, over the midnight oil, one book in a whole year, all day long and deep into the night, he is compelled to go around and hunt an audience himself, so that there may be some people who deem it worthwhile to listen, and even this costs him money. For he gets the loan of a house, prepares an auditorium, hires benches, and distributes programs.[10] And even though the reception accorded his public reading is very favorable, all that praise fades away in a day or two, like a blade of grass or a flower that has been cut, and does not come to any sure and substantial fruit, and he does not take with him from that recitation either friendship or client relationship, or any benefit that will endure in the mind of anyone, but a capricious outcry and meaningless words and fleeting pleasure. We recently praised Vespasian's generosity as being unusual and extraordinary because he had presented Bassus with the sum of 500,000 sesterces. It is indeed splendid to merit the emperor's generosity because of one's talent; but how much more splendid is it, if personal circumstances so require, that one revere oneself, make one's own genius profitable, experience one's own generosity! Add to this the fact that poets have to leave the acquaintance of friends and the charm of the city, if they wish to work out and produce anything worthy, that they must disregard other duties, and, as they themselves say, they must go off into meadows and groves,[11] that is, into solitude.

10. *Even poetry's renown is less than that of oratory. Since Maternus has talent for both, his choice is wrong.*

"Not even reputation and fame, to which alone they are devoted and which they confess is the one reward of all their labor, accrue in equal measure to poets and orators, since no one knows middling poets and few know the good ones. For when does the report of the most remarkable public readings reach the entire city? Much less common is it that the poet becomes known throughout so many provinces. How few are there who, when they have come to Rome from Spain or Asia, to say nothing about our Gauls, seek out Saleius Bassus? And, further, if anyone does seek him out, when he has once seen him, he moves on and is content, as if he had seen some painting or statue. Nor do I want this argument of mine to be understood in this way, as if I should frighten away from poetry those to whom their own natures have denied oratorical talent, if they can charm their leisure and gain reputation for their names only in this branch of studies. Indeed, I consider that all literature and all its genres are sacred and to be treated with respect, and I believe that not only your tragedy or the majesty of heroic verse but also the charm of lyrics and the playfulness of elegies and the invective of iambics

[10] See Juvenal, *Satires* 7. 38–47.
[11] The words *in nemora et lucos* are echoed by Pliny in a letter to Tacitus (9. 10. 2).

and the jesting of epigrams and whatever other form literature possesses should be preferred to all studies of other disciplines. But my dispute is with you, Maternus, because, although your nature brings you to the very citadel of eloquence, you prefer to wander off the path and, although you have obtained the greatest prizes, you dally among the more trivial. Just as, if you had been born in Greece, where it is honorable to practice athletic skills, and the gods had given you the power and strength of Nicostratus,[12] I should not permit those tremendous arms, which were born for boxing, to become puny with the lightness of the javelin or with throwing the discus, so now I summon you from auditoria and theaters into the forum to law cases and real battles, especially since you cannot even have recourse to that claim which protects many, namely, that the occupation of poets is less likely to give offense than that of orators. For the fervor of your most excellent nature waxes hot and you cause offense not for some friend but for Cato, which is more dangerous. Nor is your offense excused by the call of duty or the obligation of legal counsel or by the unwitting quality of a sudden chance remark; you seem to have chosen with forethought a character who is well known and is going to speak with authority. I realize what the response could be: tremendous expressions of approval arise from this, these things are particularly praised in the auditoria themselves and are soon discussed in everybody's conversations. Therefore do not mention the excuse of peace and security, since you are getting an opponent too great for you. For us it would be better to concern ourselves with private disputes that exist in our own age, in which, if it ever should be necessary to offend the ears of more powerful people in defense of a friend in danger, one's integrity may be approved and one's forthrightness excused."

Chapters 11–13. Maternus demurs.

11. *Maternus responds that his reputation is based upon his poetic achievements.*

When Aper had said these things with considerable vehemence, as was his custom, and in all seriousness, Maternus, relaxed and smiling, said: "Aper soothed me with a certain skill as I was preparing to mount an attack against orators that would be just as long as his praise had been, by granting those who cannot plead

---

[12] A famous athlete of the mid-first century A.D., renowned for wrestling and the *pankration*.

cases the right to write poetry. For I kept thinking that, after he had finished praising them, he would deride poets and demolish the study of poetry. However, although I can perhaps accomplish and achieve something by pleading cases, so too can I by the reading of tragedies. And I began to gain fame when I destroyed the wicked power of Vatinius, power which also debased the sacred nature of literature.[13] Today, if I have any reputation and renown, I rather think it has been acquired by the fame of my poetry than of my speeches. And I have already decided to unyoke myself from the activity of the forum, nor do I have any desire for those escorts to and from my house which you mentioned or the mobs of those who come to pay their respects, no more than for bronze medallions, which have forced their way into my home even against my will. For personal integrity does a better job than eloquence of protecting the position and safety of each person; and, except to appear in someone else's defense, I am not afraid that I shall ever have to speak in the senate.

12. *Poetry preceded oratory and has brought equal renown and even greater safety.*

"Indeed the meadows and groves and the very solitude which Aper chided afford me so much pleasure that I rank them among the outstanding rewards of poetry, because it is not composed in hustle and bustle nor with a litigant sitting before one's door nor in the midst of the mourning clothes and tears of those who are being prosecuted, but the mind goes off into pure and unsoiled locales and enjoys holy surroundings. This was the origin, this is the inner sanctum, of eloquence; ingratiating itself with mortals, it first flowed in this appearance and style into those hearts which were chaste and unpolluted by any vices: this is the way oracles spoke. For the practice of this lucrative and blood-stained oratorical eloquence is of recent vintage and sprang from bad habits and was, as you said, Aper, discovered as a weapon. But that happy age, which I may, in our custom, call golden, was totally without orators and crimes but had a large number of poets and bards, whose function was to sing of glorious deeds and not to defend wicked ones. Nor did any have greater glory or more worshipful honor, first of all with the gods, whose interpreters they were said to be and at whose banquets they were

---

[13] The incident referred to here has not been identified.

said to take part, and then with those kings who were born from the gods and were sacred; we have not learned that there was any advocate in their company but Orpheus and Linus[14] and, if you should wish to delve deeper into the past, Apollo himself. Yet, if this seems too unreal and made up, you will surely grant me this, Aper, that Homer's reputation is no less great with later generations than that of Demosthenes and that the fame of Euripides or Sophocles is not confined by narrower bounds than is that of Lysias or Hyperides. You will find more people today who carp at Cicero's renown than at Vergil's, and no published speech of Asinius or of Messalla is as famous as Ovid's *Medea* or Varius' *Thyestes*.[15]

13. *Retirement is more appealing than the active life.*

"And I shouldn't even be afraid to compare the fortune and that happy fellowship of bards with the restless and anxious life of orators. Grant that their struggles and dangers have advanced the latter to the consulship, I prefer the carefree and quiet retirement of Vergil, in which, nonetheless, he lacked neither favor with the deified Augustus nor renown among the Roman people. Letters of Augustus testify to this, as do the people themselves, who, when they had heard verses of Vergil in a theater, rose in a body and paid him respect, since he happened to be present as a spectator, as if he were Augustus. Not even in our own times would Pomponius Secundus have yielded to Domitius Afer[16] in prestige of life or lasting quality of his renown. For what do your Crispus and Marcellus, whose careers you hold up to me as examples, have in this fortune of theirs that is really desirable? Because they fear or are feared? Because, when they are asked for something every day, those to whom they do not respond quickly enough are angry? Because, all entangled in flattery, they never seem to rulers to be sufficiently subservient nor to us to be sufficiently independent? What is this very great power of theirs?

[14]Orpheus and Linus were famed bards of mythology, often coupled; see, e.g., Vergil, *Bucolics* 4. 55ff.

[15]Lysias (fifth century B.C.) and Hyperides (fourth century B.C.) were included in the canonical list of ten great Greek orators. Gaius Asinius Pollio and Marcus Valerius Messalla Corvinus were among the significant political figures of the last half of the first century B.C.; both the *Medea* and *Thyestes*, highly praised by Quintilian, are now lost. Varius was a close friend of Vergil and Horace, and one of the editors of the *Aeneid* after Vergil's death.

[16]Pomponius Secundus was the most renowned tragic poet of the mid-first century A.D., Domitius Afer a great orator under Nero.

Freedmen customarily have as much. Indeed, let "the sweet Muses," as Vergil says,[17] carry me off to those sacred places and those fountains, after I have been released from worries and cares and the necessity of doing something daily against my inclination; nor let me any more experience with dread the mad and dangerous forum and shifting glory. Let not the noise of those who come to pay their respects nor a panting freedman arouse me; let me not write my will, while uncertain of the future, to be on the safe side; let me not have more than I could leave behind to whomsoever I should wish (for some time or other my destined day will come); and let my statue by placed on my grave not gloomy and fierce in aspect but joyful and wearing a wreath, nor let anyone consult the senate or petition the emperor to honor my memory."

Chapters 14–23. Messalla enters and expresses his admiration of the ancient orators. Aper claims the superiority of "modern" orators and castigates the orators of the republic for various failings.

14. *Messalla's appearance.*

Maternus had scarcely finished, excited and, as it were, inspired, when Vipstanus Messalla entered his room and, suspecting from everyone's serious expression that there was a discussion of some significance going on among them, asked, "Have I interrupted a private deliberation at an inappropriate time, such as your consideration of some case?"

"Not at all, not at all," said Secundus, "and I rather wish that you had come sooner; for the very carefully wrought argument of our Aper would have delighted you, when he urged Maternus to devote all his talent and attention to the pleading of cases, as would have also Maternus' charming response in behalf of his poetry, which, appropriate to the defense of poets, was rather fiery and more like the product of poets than of orators."

"That conversation," Messalla said, "would indeed have given me endless pleasure, and the very fact delights me that you, men of the highest character and also the best orators of our times, practice your talents not only in the business of the forum and the study of oratory, but even carry on discussions of this kind, which sharpen the intellect and furnish the most enjoyable pleasure of learning and literature not only to yourselves who debate those questions but also to those to whose ears they

[17] *Georgics* 2. 475.

may come. Therefore, indeed, I see that you, Secundus, are to be praised, because, in writing the biography of Julius African-us,[18] you have given men the expectation of more books of this kind, just as much as Aper, because he has not yet finished with rhetorical school exercises and prefers to use his leisure in the manner of the new rhetoricians rather than of the old orators."

15. *Messalla requests one of the others to explain why present-day ora-tors are so inferior to those of earlier generations.*

Then Aper took up, "You continue, Messalla, to marvel only at what is old and ancient but to mock and scorn the culture of our own times. For I have often heard this statement of yours, when, forgetting your own eloquence and that of your brother,[19] you claimed that there was no orator at the present time who was a match for the ancients, and you said this with considerable con-fidence because, I believe, you were not afraid of being thought spiteful, since you were denying yourself the renown that others grant you."

"And I do not regret that statement of mine, nor do I believe that Secundus or Maternus or even you, Aper, have a different opinion, although you occasionally argue against it. And I should like one of you, as a favor, to investigate and explain the reasons for this tremendous difference; very often I hunt for these rea-sons myself. And what comforts certain people makes the in-quiry all the more pressing for me, since I see that it has even happened to the Greeks; for the renowned Sacerdos Nicetes or anyone else who causes Ephesus or Mytilene to quake with the audience's chorus of applause has fallen further from the level of Aeschines[20] and Demosthenes than Afer or Africanus or you yourselves have fallen from the level of Cicero or Asinius."

16. *Aper claims that Demosthenes, for example, is a "modern" orator.*

"You have raised a question that is important and worthy of dis-cussion," said Secundus. "But who will expound it more appro-priately than you, who have added careful thought to your very great learning and extraordinary talent?"

Messalla replied, "I shall reveal my thoughts to you on this condition, that you also help this presentation of mine along."

---

[18] A distinguished contemporary orator.

[19] Marcus Aquilius Regulus, his half brother, was a notorious informer.

[20] Sacerdos Nicetes was a contemporary rhetorician; Aeschines was Demos-thenes' great opponent.

"I promise this for two of us," said Maternus; "for Secundus and I will deal with those aspects of the subjects which we shall realize you have not so much omitted as left to us. A little while ago you said that it is Aper's custom to disagree and it is quite obvious that he has been ready for a long time to take the offensive and that he cannot endure with equanimity this agreement of ours regarding the praise of the ancients."

"Ah no," said Aper, "I shall not permit our age to be condemned by this conspiracy of yours without being heard and given some defense. But first I shall ask this, Whom do you call 'the ancients'? What period of orators do you mark out by that designation? For when I hear of 'the ancients,' I think of certain men of old who were born long ago, and there come before my eyes Ulysses and Nestor, whose period preceded ours by about 1,300 years; but you bring forth the names of Demosthenes and Hyperides, who, it is beyond question, flourished in the times of Philip and Alexander, and yet outlived them. From this it is clear that not much more than 300 years fall between our period and that of Demosthenes. If you should relate this span of time to the frail condition of our bodies, it would perhaps seem long; but if you consider the character of centuries and the tremendous extent of this eternity, it is very brief and close at hand. For if, as Cicero writes in his *Hortensius*,[21] that is a true and great year in which the same position of the constellations of heaven, exactly as it is now, comes again into existence, and that year embraces 12,954 of these which we call years, it begins to appear that Demosthenes, whom you put forth as old and ancient, lived not only in the same year as we do but even in the same month.

17. *Cicero lived but yesterday and could have been heard by someone still alive.*

"But I pass on to the Latin orators, among whom you are wont to prefer to the eloquent men of our times not Menenius Agrippa,[22] I think, who can seem 'ancient,' but Cicero, Caesar, Caelius, Calvus, Brutus, Asinius, and Messalla; I do not see why you assign them to ancient times rather than to ours. For, to speak about Cicero himself, he was killed, as his freedman Tiro reported, on December 7 in the year[23] which was, to be sure, that of the con-

[21] The *Hortensius* is lost, except for fragments. Written in 45, it was an invocation to the study of philosophy. It was influential in antiquity, particularly upon St. Augustine.

[22] Consul 503 B.C.; see Livy, *History of Rome* 2. 32.

[23] In 43 B.C.

sulship of Hirtius and Pansa, a year in which the deified Augustus caused himself and Quintus Pedius to be appointed suffect consuls in succession to Pansa and Hirtius. Figure fifty-six years during which the deified Augustus then governed the state; add Tiberius' twenty-three, Gaius' reign, which lasted almost four years, the fourteen years each of Claudius and Nero, that long but single year of Galba and Otho and Vitellius, and now the sixth year of this happy principate, in which Vespasian is making the commonwealth prosper; there is a sum of one hundred twenty years from the death of Cicero to the present day, the life span of one man. For I myself have seen an old man in Britain who claimed that he participated in that battle in which the Britons undertook to keep Caesar away from their shores and to drive him off when he was invading the island. And so, if captivity or personal desire or some stroke of fortune had dragged that man, who had fought against Gaius Caesar, to the city, the same man could equally well have heard Caesar himself and Cicero and also have been present at our pleadings. Indeed, at the last public largess, you yourselves saw a number of old men who related that they had again and again received a largess also from the deified Augustus. From this one can gather that both Corvinus and Asinius could have been heard by them— for Asinius lived to the middle of Augustus' principate, Corvinus almost to the very end;[24] therefore do not split an age and call orators 'old and ancient' whom the ears of the same men were able to recognize and, as it were, join together and associate with us.

18. *"Styles and manners of speech change with the times."*

"I have made these preliminary remarks for this reason, so that, if any praise accrues to the times from the renown and glory of these orators, I might show that it is the property of all and nearer to us than to Servius Galba or Gaius Carbo[25] and others whom we would properly call 'ancient'; for they are rough, graceless, crude, and inartistic. I should wish that your Calvus or Caelius or Cicero himself had not imitated them in any regard. For I wish now to proceed more vigorously and boldly, after first making this claim, that the styles and manners of speech change with the times. Thus Gaius Gracchus is more elaborate and

[24]Pollio died in A.D. 5, Corvinus in either A.D. 8 or 13, so that the statement in the text is inaccurate.
[25]Consuls 144 and 120 B.C., respectively.

richer in expression than old Cato[26] to whom he has been compared, in the same way Crassus is more polished and ornate than Gracchus, thus Cicero is more luminous and refined and impassioned than either, Corvinus is milder and more pleasing and more precise in his choice of words than Cicero. And I do not ask who was the most eloquent: I am content to have shown this for now, that there is no single aspect of eloquence, but that also in those whom you call 'ancient' a number of kinds are to be discerned, nor is that which is different at once worse, but, as the result of the vice of human envy, old things are always praised and those of the present day held in scorn. We do not doubt, do we, that people have been found who admired Appius Claudius[27] in preference to Cato? There is no question that even Cicero had his detractors, to whom he seemed swollen, inflated, not terse enough, extravagant in his rhythms, redundant, and insufficiently Attic.[28] At any rate you have read letters of Calvus and Brutus which were sent to Cicero, from which it is easy to gather that Calvus seemed to Cicero bloodless and feeble, while Brutus appeared dull and disjointed; on the other hand, Cicero was criticized by Calvus as being weak and effeminate, and by Brutus, to quote his words, 'because he was feeble and lame.' If you ask me, all seem to have spoken the truth. But I shall soon come to them as individuals, now I have to deal with them all.

19. *An orator must have a new and exciting style to avoid boring his listeners.*

"For since the worshippers of the ancients are accustomed to set up this boundary of 'antiquity,' as it were, I claim that Cassius Severus,[29] whom they attack on the grounds that he was the first one to turn from that old and straightforward path of speaking, changed to that kind of speech not because of lack of talent or inadequate training in literature but by sane judgment and un-

[26] Gaius Gracchus was tribune in 123–122 B.C. Cato was consul in 195 and censor in 184.

[27] Appius Claudius Caecus (the blind), censor 312 B.C., constructed the Via Appia and the Aqua Appia.

[28] The devotees of the "Asianist" school sought florid and extravagant effects, the "Atticists" cultivated plainness and simplicity. Cicero claimed, as an eclectic, to avoid the ills of both styles.

[29] Born about the middle of the first century B.C., Cassius Severus was banished by Augustus for his wanton attacks upon the aristocracy. His exile was continued, under harsher conditions because of his unrepentant nature, by Tiberius; he died in A.D. 32.

derstanding. For he saw, as I said a little while ago, that the manner and style of speech had to be changed to accompany the change in the times and the difference in taste. That earlier people, inexperienced and uncultured, easily endured the tedious presentation of the most long-winded speeches and used to applaud it as an achievement if anyone used up a day in speaking. Indeed, the lengthy preparatory introductions and the far-fetched presentation of argument and the display of many divisions and a thousand levels of proofs and whatever else is prescribed in the dry-as-dust books of Hermagoras and Apollodorus[30] were honored; but if anyone seemed to have sniffed philosophy and inserted some commonplace from it into his speech, his praises rang to heaven. And it was not surprising; for these things were new and unfamiliar, and also very few of the orators themselves knew the precepts of rhetoricians or the principles of philosophers. But, goodness knows, when all these things have become public property, when scarcely anyone stands in the audience who, though not fully trained, has surely become acquainted with the basic elements of these disciplines, we need new and exciting styles of eloquence, by means of which the orator may avoid boring his listeners, particularly before judges, who hear cases by their authority and power of office, not because of their knowledge of the legal code or the laws, and do not accept the length of time proposed for speaking but set it themselves and hold that one should not have to wait for an orator until he decides to speak about the subject at hand, but often on their own admonish him and call him back when he is wandering elsewhere, and claim that they are in a hurry.

20. *Present-day style is more beautiful and polished.*

"Who will now tolerate an orator who speaks first about his poor health? That's the way Corvinus' introductions are, almost without exception. Who will wait out five books against Verres? Who will suffer through those lengthy speeches about defendants' pleas and rules of procedure which we read in behalf of Marcus Tullius or Aulus Caecina?[31] At this time the judge anticipates the speaker and becomes hostile to him unless he has been won

[30]Rhetoricians of the second and first centuries B.C., respectively.
[31]Cicero's successful prosecution of Verres occurred in 70 B.C. Aper fails to note that only the first speech was delivered, with the rest being published as pamphlets after Verres fled into exile. The defenses of Tullius and Caecina took place in 72 or 71 and 69, respectively.

over and seduced by the flow of evidence or the brilliance of
thoughts or the shining glitter of descriptions. Also the mob of
bystanders and the chance listener who wanders in and out
have become accustomed now to demand richness and beauty
in a speech, nor does anyone tolerate a somber and unpolished
old-fashionedness in the courts any more than if someone should
wish to reproduce the gestures of Roscius or Ambivius Turpio[32]
on the stage. Now indeed young men, namely those who are
still on the threshold of knowledge and who attach themselves
to orators to improve themselves, want not only to hear but also
to bring home something remarkable and worthy of recollection;
and they pass it on among themselves and often write it to their
communities and provinces if some thought has glittered because of a concise and striking saying or a passage has shone
because of its careful poetic dress. For even the beauty of poetry
is now required of the orator, a beauty not defiled by the old rot
of Accius or Pacuvius[33] but drawn from the shrine of Horace and
Vergil and Lucan. By paying deference to the taste and judgment of these people, then, the present age of orators has developed, more beautiful and more polished. And our speeches are
not for this reason any less effective, since they give pleasure to
the judges' ears. Tell me now whether you believe the temples of
these times less solidly built, since they are constructed not of
rough stones and shapeless tiles but gleam with marble and
glow with gold?

21. *Ancient orators were tedious and crude.*

"Indeed, I shall make a simple confession to you: in the case of
some of the ancients, I scarcely keep myself from laughing, and,
in the case of others, from sleeping. And I do not speak of one of
the rank and file, Canutius or Attius, to say nothing about Fur-
nius and Toranius and the others whom these bones and this
wasting-away prove to be residents of the same sickroom. Calvus himself, although, I think, he left behind twenty-one orations, hardly satisfies me in one or two little speeches. And I see
that others do not disagree with this judgment of mine; for how
few are there who read Calvus' speeches against Asicius or
Drusus? But, to be sure, the speeches he delivered against Vati-

---

[32] Famous actors of the first and second centuries B.C., respectively.

[33] The best-known of Roman tragedians; Pacuvius died in 132 B.C., Accius in
about 86 B.C.

nius, and especially the second of these, are taken in hand by all those concerned with oratory;[34] for it is ornate in its words and expressions and gauged to the ears of his audience, so that one knows that Calvus too knew what was better and that he lacked not the inclination to keep him from speaking more loftily and elegantly but rather the talent and the power. And to continue. With Caelius' speeches, certainly those give pleasure, either completely or in part, in which we recognize the brilliance and loftiness of our own times. However, his commonplace expressions and construction full of hiatus and crude periods[35] reek of the old days; and I am sure that no one is so much of an antiquarian that he applauds Caelius whenever he is an 'ancient.'[36] Let us indeed grant Gaius Caesar that he accomplished less in the field of oratory than his unique genius demanded of him because of the greatness of his enterprises and because he was too busy, just as we should leave Brutus to his philosophy; for even his admirers admit that he fell short of his reputation in his speeches. Perhaps no one reads Caesar's speech in behalf of Decidius the Samnite, or Brutus' for King Deiotarus, and others of similarly uninspired dullness, except a person who marvels at their poetry. For they also composed poems and had them included in libraries; they were not better poets than Cicero, but they are luckier, since fewer people realize that they wrote poetry.[37] Asinius too, although he was born in times nearer ours, seems to me to have studied among men like Menenius and Appius.[38] He certainly reproduced Pacuvius and Accius in his speeches as well as in his tragedies: he is so tough and dry. But, just as a man's body, so precisely is that speech beautiful in which the veins do not stick out and the bones cannot be counted but rather temperate and healthy blood fills the limbs and swells in the muscles and a glow coats the sinews themselves and an elegance graces them. I do not wish to attack Corvinus, since the fault was not his own, not to express the richness and glitter of

[34] All those above mentioned were orators of the first century B.C.; Calvus' speeches remain only in fragments.

[35] Hiatus refers to breaks between words where sounds would normally coalesce. Periods are sentences or clauses which express complete thoughts.

[36] The speeches of Caelius are not extant, nor are those of Caesar and Brutus, mentioned below. Caelius was a friend of Cicero.

[37] This is not a completely fair judgment. In his youth, according to Plutarch, *Cicero* 2.3–4, Cicero was considered the leading poet of Rome. His reputation suffered from some unfortunate and self-centered lines written about his consulship; see Quintilian, 10. 1.24, and Juvenal, *Satires* 10. 122ff.

[38] See footnotes 22 and 27.

our times; and we see how little his imaginative or creative ability supported his critical judgment.

22. *Cicero too had the same battle. His own style is polished and elegant.*

"I come to Cicero, who had the same battle with his contemporaries that I have with you. For they admired the ancients,[39] he himself preferred the eloquence of his own times; nor does he excel the orators of the same age in anything more than in taste. For he was the first one to apply a finish to a speech, the first one to follow a principle of selection in vocabulary and to produce skillful arrangement, and he also attempted flowery passages and came upon certain aphorisms, especially in those speeches he composed when he was already an old man and near the end of his life, that is, after he had become more proficient and had learned, by experience and practice, what the best type of oratory was. For his earlier speeches are not without the faults of the old days: he moves slowly in his introductions, is long-winded in his narratives, wearisome in his digressions; he plods along and rarely gets excited; few sentences come to an end with rhythm and with some brilliance. You could excerpt nothing, take nothing away with you, and, just as in a rudely constructed building, the wall is certainly strong and going to last, yet it is inadequately polished and shining. I, however, want an orator, just as a rich and tasteful head of a household, to be sheltered not only by the kind of home that keeps away the rain and wind, but even one that delights the eye; and I wish him to be possessed not only of furniture that is adequate for ordinary purposes, but gold and jewels should be among his belongings, so that he may more often get pleasure from handling and gazing upon them. Further, certain things should be avoided as already passé and dated: let no word be tainted with blight, so to speak; let no sentence be composed, in the style of a chronicler, with a tedious and lifeless arrangement; let the orator avoid foul and witless scurrility, let him vary his manner of writing, and let him not have all his sentences end in one and the same rhythmical pattern.[40]

23. *Contemporary orators display beautiful style.*

"I do not wish to mock 'the wheel of Fortune' and 'pork sauce'

---

[39] The Attic orators of Greece.

[40] Prose rhythm was very important to the ancients, particularly at the end of a sentence, the *clausula*.

and that phrase 'it would appear to be,'[41] the stock ending, by way of reflection, of every other sentence in all his speeches. For I have unwillingly recalled these and have omitted more, which nonetheless are the only things those who call themselves 'ancient orators' admire and therefore reproduce. I shall mention no one by name, since I am content to have indicated the class of men; but undoubtedly they pass before your eyes, people who read Lucilius in preference to Horace, and Lucretius rather than Vergil, who consider the eloquent style of Aufidius Bassus or Servilius Nonianus inferior to that of Sisenna or Varro,[42] who despise the written speeches of our rhetoricians and marvel at those of Calvus. Those who babble before a judge in the old-fashioned way are heeded by no audience, not heard by the people, scarcely endured, to top it off, by the person involved in the case: being so dismal and uncouth, they gain that very state of good health of which they boast not by vigor but by fasting. Further, not even in the case of the body do doctors approve sound health that comes about because of emotional trouble; it is not enough for one not to be sick: I want him to be strong, high-spirited, vigorous. He is not far removed from indisposition in whom only soundness of body is praised. You indeed, you very eloquent men, as you can and as you do, give luster to our age by the most beautiful style of oratory. For I see you, Messalla, imitating all the most expressive aspects of the ancients, and you, Maternus and Secundus, mingle the shining glitter of vocabulary with weightiness of thought in such a way, such is the choice of subject matter, such the order of material, such the richness, whenever the case demands it, such the brevity, whenever it is permitted, such the grace of composition, such the clarity of thought, such the manner in which you express your emotions and control your outspokenness, that even if ill will and envy warped our judgments, our posterity would speak the truth about you."

Chapters 24–35. Maternus invites Messalla to explain the inferiority of recent oratory. Messalla defends the ancients and then considers why oratory has declined over the last century. The answer is the inferiority of modern education and training.

---

[41] Mentioned here are three typical Ciceronian expressions or puns.

[42] Lucilius (second century B.C.) was considered the father of Roman satire. Aufidius and Servilius lived in the first century A.D., Sisenna and Varro in the first century B.C.; all four were historians, although the polymath Varro embraced many fields and was considered the most learned of Romans.

24. *Maternus asks Messalla to explain why modern orators are so inferior to the ancients.*

When Aper had finished speaking, Maternus said: "Do you recognize the fire and enthusiasm of our Aper? With what a flood and passion he defended our age! How fully and extensively he tore the ancients to shreds! With what genius and inspiration, not to mention learning and skill, he borrowed from them those very weapons with which he then attacked them! Nonetheless, Messalla, he should not cause you to break your promise. For we do not need a defender of the ancients nor do we compare any one of ourselves, although we have just been praised, with those whom Aper assailed. That is not even his own opinion, but, in line with an old practice often approved by our philosophers, he took for himself the role of the opposition. Therefore give us, not praise of the ancients (for their reputation praises them sufficiently), but the reasons why we have fallen so short of their eloquence, and that too although chronology has shown that there have passed only one hundred and twenty years from the death of Cicero up to the present."

25. *Messalla grants that the ancients differed among themselves, but the age of Cicero is rightly recognized as the greatest among the Romans.*

Messalla replied: "I shall follow the course you have laid out, Maternus; for one does not have to spend much time refuting Aper, who first of all, to my mind, stirred up a dispute about nomenclature, on the grounds that they who beyond any question lived one hundred years ago were inappropriately called 'ancients.' However, I am not going to fight about a word; let him call them 'ancients' or 'elders' or by whatever other name he prefers, provided that everyone knows that the eloquence of those times was loftier. I do not even argue against that part of his discussion, to keep from confessing that numerous types of oratory existed even in the same ages, much less in different ones. But, just as first place among the Attic orators is assigned to Demosthenes and Aeschines, Hyperides, Lysias, and Lycurgus occupy the next rank, and, nonetheless, this age of orators is given especial and unanimous approval, so, among us, Cicero indeed excelled the other eloquent men of the time, and, on the other hand, Calvus, Asinius, Caesar, Caelius, and Brutus are rightly preferred to their predecessors and successors. Nor does the fact that they differ one from the other in particular details have any significance, since they agree in general characteristics. Calvus is more concise, Asinius more energetic, Caesar more brilliant, Caelius more biting, Brutus more serious, Cicero more vigorous and rich and powerful: all nonetheless display the same healthiness of eloquence, so that, if you should take into your hand the orations of all of them at the same time, you would know that there was a certain similarity and relationship of taste and intent, in spite of variation of talent. As to the fact that they reproached each other and that some comments were included in their letters that displayed their mutual ill will, this is a fault not of orators but of human beings. For I believe that Calvus and Asinius and Cicero himself were accustomed to hate and envy and to be afflicted with the other faults of human frailty; I think that of these only Brutus revealed his innermost convictions straightforwardly and honestly, without being influenced by ill will and envy. Can it be that he envied Cicero, he who seems to me to have envied not even Caesar? What is said with regard to Servius Galba and Gaius Laelius and any others of the still older generation, whom Aper did not cease to attack, does not need an advocate, since I admit that their eloquence lacked certain qualities, because it was still growing and had not yet reached maturity.

26. *Even a crude style is superior to artificiality and wantonness.*

"But if, after eliminating that best and most ideal type of oratory, a style of speech must be chosen, I should indeed prefer the impetuosity of Gaius Gracchus or the ripe eloquence of Lucius Crassus to the artificial flourishes of Maecenas or the jinglings of Gallio: [43] it is so much better to clothe a speech even in a rough toga than to make it stand out with the colored clothes of a courtesan. For the practice is inappropriate for an orator and even less for a man, although it is the vogue among many speakers of our times, to reproduce the rhythms of the stage by wanton language and shallow thoughts and lax structure. And many boast, as proof of their renown and glory and genius, that their works are sung and danced to, a thing which it should shock them even to hear. From this there stems that shameful and absurd, but nonetheless common, statement, that our orators are said to speak lasciviously, our actors to dance eloquently. Indeed I would not deny that Cassius Severus, whom alone our Aper

[43] Lucius Crassus was a statesman and orator of the second and first centuries b.c. and was much admired by Cicero. Maecenas was the minister of Augustus and the patron of Vergil and Horace. Gallio, a friend of Seneca the Elder, is particularly known to us because he presided at the trial of the Apostle Paul (*Acts* 18:12).

dared mention,[44] if he were compared with those who lived after him, could be called an 'orator,' although in a large part of his output he displays more bile than blood. For he is the first one who, paying no attention to the order of his material and ignoring moderation and decorum of vocabulary, unskilled even in the use of his own weapons and often thrown off his balance by his eagerness to strike a blow, does not fight but wages a brawl. But, as I said, compared with those who follow him, in breadth of learning, charm of wit, and power of intellect itself, he much surpasses the rest, none of whom Aper deigned to name and, as it were, bring into the battle. But I anticipated that, when he had leveled his charge at Asinius and Caelius and Calvus, he would present us with another battalion and mention most of their names or, at least, enough of them to enable us to set one against Cicero, another against Caesar, and finally one against one all the way. Now, however, content with having attacked the reputations of the ancient orators by name, he did not dare to praise anyone of their successors except in very general terms, since he was afraid, I suppose, of offending many by picking out a few. For how few professional rhetoricians are there who do not flatter themselves by imagining that they rank ahead of Cicero but clearly behind Gabinianus?[45] But I shall not hesitate to name individuals, so that it may more easily be evident, by giving instances, by what steps eloquence has declined and deteriorated."

27. *Maternus reminds Messalla of the need to explain why past eloquence is superior.*

"Let that pass," said Maternus, "and rather keep your promise. For we do not need this proven, that the ancients were better speakers, which is obvious to me, but we seek the reasons, which you said a little while back that you were accustomed to discuss, when you were clearly in a better mood and less provoked with the eloquence of our times, before Aper made you mad by attacking your ancestors."

"I was not angered," he said, "by the argument of my good friend Aper, and it will not be proper for you to be angered if anything perhaps grates upon your ears, since you know that this is the ground rule for discussions of this type, to express one's opinion without any loss of good will."

[44] See footnote 29.

[45] An older contemporary of Quintilian; St. Jerome ranked him with Cicero and Quintilian.

"Go on then," said Maternus, "and since you are speaking about the men of old, use the old freedom of speech, from which we have fallen further than from their eloquence."

28. *The cause lies in the upbringing and education of the young.*

Messalla began: "You are seeking, Maternus, causes that are not hidden from view nor unknown either to yourself or to Secundus here or Aper, even if you assign me the task of discussing things we all know. For who does not realize that eloquence and other arts have declined from that ancient renown not because of the incapacity of men, but because of the laziness of the young, the lack of concern of their parents, the ignorance of professors, and the disregard of old practice? The evils that first arose in Rome soon spread throughout Italy and now flow into the provinces. Yet your provinces [46] are better known to you: I shall speak about the city and about our own home-grown vices, which immediately embrace children at birth and are compounded at every stage of life; I shall first say a few words about our ancestors' stern discipline in bringing up and training their children. For in the past each man's child, borne by a chaste mother, was reared not in the room of a nursemaid who had been bought but in the bosom and embrace of his mother; it was her particular merit to supervise the home and be devoted to the children. However, if need arose, some older female relation was chosen, to whose proven and tried character all the young of the same family were entrusted; it was a terrible thing to say anything in her presence that seemed obscene or to do anything that seemed disgraceful. And the mother supervised not only the children's studies and school exercises but also their recreations and play with noteworthy integrity and modesty. It was in this way, we have learned, that Cornelia, the mother of the Gracchi, Aurelia, the mother of Caesar, and Atia, the mother of Augustus, oversaw their upbringing and raised their distinguished sons. This discipline and stern training had this object, that the character of each, sound, wholesome, and unwarped by bad habits, might at once embrace honorable pursuits with absolute devotion and, whether inclined to military life or to jurisprudence or to the study of oratory, might do that alone and drink it in totally.

[46] Aper, Secundus, and perhaps Maternus were natives of Gaul. Messalla was the only native-born Roman.

29. *Children are raised by worthless people and exposed to misbehavior and vice.*

"But, as it is now, the child, while still unable to speak, is entrusted to some worthless Greek maid, who has the assistance of one or at most two of all the slaves, and they are generally the ones of poorest character and unsuited for any important duty. Straightway the children's pliable and unmolded minds are imbued with their nursery tales and superstitions; and no one in the whole household has any concern for what he says or does in the presence of his master's child. Even more, the parents themselves do not accustom their young to honesty and good conduct, but to naughtiness and rowdiness, through which there gradually creep in impudence and contempt for one's self as well as for someone else. Now indeed the special and unique vices of this city seem to me to be conceived almost in the mother's womb, namely enthusiasm for the stage and passion for gladiators and horse racing: how little room does a mind busied and obsessed with these things leave for good pursuits? How few will you find who speak of anything else at home? What other discussions of young men do we hear whenever we enter the lecture halls? Not even the schoolmasters speak of anything else more frequently with their pupils; for they attract students not by the strictness of the training they offer or their proven talent but by calling upon potential students to pay their respects and by tricks of flattery.

30. *The old orators were learned and experienced in all subjects.*

"I pass over the first stages of education, at which level too they do not work hard enough: insufficient effort is devoted to reading authors and unrolling the pages of the past and learning the branches of knowledge, human nature, and real events. But those whom they call rhetoricians are sought out; it is my intention to explain right away when their profession was first introduced into this city and how they were without influence among our ancestors, but I must recall our minds to that training that we have learned those orators followed, whose endless labor and daily practice and continual studies in every branch of their disciplines are displayed even in their books. Surely Cicero's essay entitled *Brutus* is known to you, in the last part of which (the first part contains a survey of the old orators) he relates his own beginnings and stages of advancement, the development, so to speak, of his own eloquence: he tells that he learned civil law from Quintus Mucius and drank in deeply all the branches of philosophy from Philo the Academic and Diodotus the Stoic,[47] and that, not content with those teachers who were available to him in the city, he also traveled through Achaea and Asia,[48] to embrace the entire range of all the arts. And so, goodness knows, one becomes aware in Cicero's works that he lacked the knowledge neither of geometry nor of music nor of philology nor, to sum up, of any liberal art. He had learned the subtle skill of dialectic, the practical lessons of ethics, the movements and causes of natural events. This, gentlemen, this is the result: that remarkable eloquence rushes forth and overflows from extensive learning and very many achievements and knowledge that is universal; for the function and activity of an orator are not confined within narrow and restricted limits, as are those of other skills, but that man is an orator who can discourse about every subject nobly, elegantly, and persuasively, in accordance with the loftiness of the subject, making proper use of occasions, and producing pleasure in his audience.

31. *They did not declaim in the schools of rhetoricians but became broadly knowledgeable about moral subjects.*

"Those men of old had become convinced of this, they realized that to accomplish this there was need, not of declaiming in the schools of the rhetoricians nor of exercising tongue and voice in debates fictitious and totally unrelated to reality, but of filling their minds with those fields of knowledge with which debate is carried on about things good and evil, about the honorable and dishonorable, about the just and the unjust; for this is the subject matter that an orator must discuss. For in the courts our general subject is equity, in senate deliberations expediency, in panegyrics moral integrity, but in such a way that often these precise subjects are intermingled: no one can speak fully, without monotony, and elegantly about them unless he has learned human nature, the meaning of virtues, the depravity of vices, and has gotten an understanding of those traits that fall in the categories neither of virtues nor vices. From these sources flow even the following skills, so that he who knows what anger is may more easily arouse or calm the anger of a judge, and he who knows

[47] Quintus Mucius Scaevola, the augur, like his cousin of the same name, the pontifex, was among the leading legal scholars of the second and first centuries B.C. He lived from about 159 to 88. Philo came to Rome in 88. Diodotus was an intimate friend of Cicero.

[48] These were the Roman provinces, the former including Athens, the latter the great cities of the coast of Asia Minor.

what pity is and by what emotions of the mind it is stirred up
may more readily lead a judge to pity. An orator trained in these
skills and practices, whether he will have to speak among people
who are hostile or biased or envious or sullen or frightened, will
feel the pulse of their moods and will treat the case and temper
his speech in accordance with the requirement of each listener's
character, since every tool has been prepared and held in reserve for every emergency. There are those among whom a manner of speaking which is concise and succinct and which immediately brings each and every argument to a conclusion gains
more credence: with these attention given to logic[49] will be profitable. Others get greater pleasure from a speech smoothly and
steadily drawn from the common emotions: to win these over
we will borrow arguments from the Peripatetics which are suitable and ready at hand for every discussion. The Academics will
furnish combativeness, Plato sublimity, Xenophon charm; it will
not be inappropriate for the orator to have at his disposal certain
moral maxims even of Epicurus and Metrodorus[50] and to use
them as the situation demands. For we are not molding a phi-
losopher or a devotee of the Stoics, but a man who ought to
drink deeply of certain studies and taste all. And for this reason
the orators of old understood civil law and were trained in philology, music, and geometry. For cases occur, and this is almost
always the circumstance, in which knowledge of law is demanded, and there are also some in which the last-named disciplines are necessary.

32. *Present-day orators are, in contrast, shallow and ignorant.*

"Nor should anyone reply that it is sufficient that we be taught
something superficial and simple for an emergency. For, first of
all, we make use of our own possessions in one way and of borrowed things in another, and it is clear that there is a vast difference whether one possesses or borrows what he displays. Then,
a wide range of culture, of itself, gives us distinction even when
we are handling other material and shines forth and stands out
where you would least expect it. And not only the learned and
sagacious listener but even the people realize this and at once

[49]The Stoics excelled in logic.

[50]Epicureanism was considered unworthy of the orator's attention in the latter
days of the republic. Metrodorus was a disciple of Epicurus. Epicureanism urged
the primacy of pleasure and nonparticipation in public affairs. Stoicism was
more attractive to the Romans because service to the state fit well with its belief
in living the best and most ethical life, in accordance with reason.

deck him with such praise that they confess that he has properly
devoted himself to his studies, that he has advanced through all
the stages of eloquence, that, in short, he is an orator; I claim
that he cannot arise in any other way and never has arisen unless he is one who has gone forth into the forum armed with all
the arts as if, equipped with all weapons, he were going into
battle. This is so neglected by the speakers of the present that we
discern in their pleadings the shocking and disgusting errors
even of our everyday speech; a further result is that they are ignorant of the laws, do not have knowledge of the decrees of the
senate, go so far as to mock prescriptive law, and, indeed, totally
reject the study of philosophy and the maxims of wise men.
They cram their eloquence into very few commonplace expressions and cramped epigrams as if it had been expelled from its
kingdom, so that oratory, once the mistress of all the arts that
filled men's breasts with a most magnificent retinue, now, pruned
and shorn, without adornment, without high state, I should almost say without independence, is learned as if it were one of
the vulgar occupations. I think that this is the first and foremost
reason why we have fallen so far short of the eloquence of the
ancient orators. If witnesses are demanded, whom shall I name
of greater influence among the Greeks than Demosthenes, who,
tradition has it, was a most attentive student of Plato? And
Cicero reports, more or less in these words, that, whatever his
achievement in oratory, he accomplished it not in the workshops
of the rhetoricians but in the open spaces of the Academy.[51]
There are other reasons, important and weighty, which should
properly be discussed by you, since I indeed have now done my
duty and have, as is my custom, given sufficient offense to
many, who I am sure will say, if perchance they will have heard
of these remarks, that I applauded my own foolish pursuits
while praising the knowledge of law and philosophy as essential
for an orator."

33. *Practical experience used to be joined to knowledge.*

And Maternus said: "You still seem to me to be so far from having finished the task you undertook that you seem only to have
begun and to have given certain traces and outlines, as it were.
For you told us in what arts the orators of old were customarily
trained and you pointed out the difference between our laziness

---

[51] The Academy in Athens was the site of Plato's school. The reference is
probably to Cicero, *Orator* 3. 12.

and ignorance and their most vigorous and fruitful studies: I am waiting for what follows, so that, just as I learned from you what they knew or we do not know, I may also learn this, by what kinds of practice those who were still young men and were going to make a career in the forum customarily strengthened and fostered their talents. For you will not deny, I think, that eloquence consists not only of theoretical knowledge but much more of natural ability and practice, and our friends seem, by their expressions, to indicate the same view."

Then, when both Aper and Secundus had agreed, Messalla continued, as if beginning anew, "Since I seem to have shown sufficiently the beginnings and the seeds of the eloquence of old by pointing out in what branches of knowledge the ancient orators were customarily instructed and educated, I shall now go through their practical exercises. Of course, practice is involved in the theoretical studies and no one can understand so many subjects so abstruse and so varied, unless preparation be added to knowledge, ability to preparation, and experience to ability. From this follows the conclusion that the method of mastering material to deliver and of delivering what you have mastered is the same. But if these points seem too unclear to anyone and he separates knowledge from practice, he will certainly grant the following, that the mind which has been trained in these arts and is full of them will come with far greater preparation to those practical exercises which are held to be peculiarly characteristic of orators.

34. *In times past a young man attended some distinguished orator and thereby gained a broad experience of the courts and political life.*

"And so, among our ancestors, that young man who was being readied for forensic oratory, already molded by firm upbringing at home and filled with liberal studies, was taken by his father or by relatives to some orator who held a ranking position in the commonwealth. He became accustomed to attend upon this man and to escort him and to be present at all his public utterances, whether in the law courts or in public assemblies, in such a way that he also heard his disputes and was present at his quarrels and, if I may say so, learned battle in a battle. The young men at once obtained much experience from this, a good deal of confidence, and a tremendous amount of good judgment, since they were gaining an education in broad daylight and in the midst of conflicts themselves, where no one says anything stupidly or contradictorily without suffering the penalty of having the judge reject it, his opponent cast it back into his teeth, and finally his own supporters scorn it. And so they were at once trained in real and genuine eloquence; and although they were attached to one man, they nonetheless made the acquaintance of all the advocates of the same period in a very large number of civil and criminal cases; and they had opportunity to test the differing tastes of the people themselves, from which they easily realized what was in each instance approved or rejected. In this way they did not lack a teacher, and he indeed the best and most choice, to furnish the true appearance, not a phantom, of eloquence; nor did they lack opponents and rivals who fought with swords rather than with wooden staffs, or an audience, always full and always changing, made up of friends and foes, so that nothing said, whether well or badly, could be covered up. For you know that the great and enduring reputation of oratory is won no less among the benches of opponents than among one's own; nay more, it springs more surely from that source, there it is more firmly strengthened. And, indeed, that young man about whom we are speaking, under tutors of this kind, a student of orators, a listener in the forum, an adherent of the courts, molded and trained by the experiences of others, to whom laws were known, since he heard them daily, to whom the faces of the judges were not unfamiliar, who had much experience in public assemblies, who had often tested the likes and dislikes of the people, whether he had undertaken a prosecution or a defense, was at once, himself alone, equal to any case. Lucius Crassus was eighteen years old when he prosecuted Gaius Carbo with a speech which even today we read with admiration; so too, with speeches just as lasting, Caesar, aged twenty, prosecuted Dolabella, Asinius Pollio was twenty-one when he attacked Gaius Cato, and Calvus, when he was only a little older than that, prosecuted Vatinius.

35. *Nowadays the young practice speaking in the schools of the rhetoricians.*

"But now our young men are taken to the schools of those who are called rhetoricians; it is clear from the following that they existed a little before Cicero's times and found no favor with our ancestors, because, as Cicero says, they were ordered by the censors Crassus and Domitius to close 'a school of impudence.'[52]

---

[52] A decree of the senate banished rhetoricians and philosophers in 161 B.C. The censorship of Crassus and Domitius was in 92.

But, as I had begun to say, they are brought to the schools, where I should find it hard to say whether the place itself or their fellow students or the character of their studies do their abilities greater damage. For there is no sense of respect in a place that no one enters unless he is as ignorant as the teacher; there is no advantage in one's fellow students, since boys speak and are heard among boys, and young men among young men, with equal complacency; indeed, the very kinds of practice are to a large degree harmful. For, as you all know, two types of subject matter are used by rhetoricians, deliberative speeches and debates.[53] Of these the former, indeed, as if obviously rather unimportant and requiring less judgment, are assigned to boys, the debates are entrusted to the more mature, but, in faith, what they are like and how unbelievably put together! Furthermore, bombastic delivery is employed for a subject unrelated to reality. In this way it happens that they declaim in grandiose style about the rewards of tyrannicides or the choices open to women who have been raped or the remedies of pestilence or the incests committed by mothers or whatever is being discussed daily in school but rarely or never in the forum: when they come to real judges . . ."

[Here follows a gap in the manuscript, which embraced the end of Messalla's speech and the beginning of Maternus', who is the final speaker.]

Chapters 36–42. Maternus is now speaking. He focuses upon the changed political climate of the principate: with the emperor responsible for all major decisions, there is no occasion for great oratory.

36. *Maternus argues that great eloquence can exist only in a disordered state.*

"[The ancient orator] was able to think out his subject and was incapable of saying anything insignificant or trivial. Great eloquence, like a flame, is fed by fuel, is excited by motion, and grows bright as it burns. The same circumstance promoted the eloquence of the ancients in this state too. For although the orators of the present have also obtained those rewards which were properly granted in a well-ordered, peaceful, and prosperous commonwealth, those nonetheless clearly acquired greater personal advantages from that disorder and lawlessness, since, when everything was in a state of confusion and lacked a single

---

[53] These are the well-known *suasoriae* and *controversiae*.

overseer, each orator was considered as wise as the errant people could be convinced that he was. From such conditions came a continuous series of laws and consequent popularity, from such the meetings called by magistrates who almost spent the night on the rostra, from such the prosecutions of influential individuals and the feuds that were the legacy of whole families, from such the divisions within the aristocracy and the never-ending struggles of the senate against the common people. Although these, every one of them, tore the state to pieces, they nonetheless whetted the eloquence of those times and seemed to heap great rewards upon it, since, the more influential each man was in oratory, the more easily he attained public offices, gained preeminence over his colleagues in those offices, won greater influence among the leading men of the state, greater prestige in the senate, greater reputation and renown among the people. These men were the patrons even of numerous foreign peoples, these men were honored by governors on the verge of departing for their provinces and esteemed by them after their return, these men seemed to be beckoned, with no effort on their part, by praetorships and consulates, these men were not without influence even when they held no public office, since they guided the people and the senate by their advice and prestige. Nay more, they had convinced themselves that no one could rise in the state or maintain a position of importance and prominence without oratorical ability. Nor was this strange, since they were brought onto the rostra before the people even against their wills, since it was ineffectual to express an opinion briefly in the senate unless each person supported his view with ability and eloquence, since they had to reply with their own voices to the summons of some slander or legal charge, since they were required to give testimony face to face in public cases as well, not by affidavit while in absentia. Thus, great necessity was added to the very great rewards of eloquence, and, just as it was considered honorable and glorious to be thought to be a good speaker, so on the contrary it was considered disgraceful to be dumb and tongue-tied.

37. *The great political figures of the late republic were all skilled speakers.*

"They were therefore aroused by shame no less than by rewards that they not be ranked among clients rather than among patrons, that connections handed down by their ancestors not pass over to others, that they not fail to obtain public offices on the grounds of indolence and incapacity or perform them inadequately once obtained. I do not know whether there have come into your hands these old records, which still exist in the libraries of lovers of antiquity and which are just at present being collected by Mucianus,[54] and have now been arranged and published in eleven books of *Transactions*, I think, and three of *Letters*. From these it can be learned that Gnaeus Pompey and Marcus Crassus were influential not only because of their military prowess but also because of their oratorical genius; that men like the Lentuli and Metelli and Luculli and Curios[55] and the rest of the band of the aristocracy devoted much effort and attention to these studies, and that no one in those times attained great power without some eloquence or other. In addition, there was the high rank of the defendants and the importance of the issues, which of themselves are in the highest degree conducive to eloquence. For it makes a great deal of difference whether you have to speak about a theft or rules of procedure and an injunction, or about corruption at elections, the plundering of allies, and the murder of citizens. Just as it is better that these evils not occur and that we should possess that best kind of state in which we suffer no such thing, yet, when they occurred, they furnished great material for eloquence. For the power of genius grows with the importance of affairs, nor can anyone produce a speech that is brilliant and renowned unless he has found a case worthy of it. The speeches that Demosthenes composed against his guardians do not, I think, give him luster, nor do the defenses of Publius Quinctius or Licinius Archias make Cicero a great orator: Catiline and Milo and Verres and Antony[56] have given him this reputation; not that it would be of such great importance for the state to produce bad citizens so that orators might have richer material for delivery, but, as I continually remind you, let us remember our inquiry and know that we speak about that art which existed more easily in violent and uneasy times. Who does not know that it is more advantageous and better to enjoy peace than to be assailed by war? Nevertheless, wars produce more good soldiers than does peace. The situation with eloquence is similar. For the more often it has stood in the

---

[54] Gaius Licinius Mucianus, governor of Syria at the end of Nero's reign, supported Vespasian in the latter's claim of the principate; indeed, he may well have instigated that claim. Three times consul (66, 70, 72), he was until his death, sometime between 75 and 77, an important figure in Vespasian's government. See *Agricola* 7.

[55] These were were all contemporaries of Cicero.

[56] These speeches all survive.

line of battle, as it were, and the more blows it has delivered and received and the greater the adversaries and the more bitter the battles it has deliberately chosen, so much the more is it, in public report, loftier, more distinguished, and ennobled by the very trials it has endured; the nature of men is such that they wish to gaze at the dangers of others while themselves free from care.[57]

38. *Law courts then furnished opportunity for great oratory.*

"I pass to the characteristics and custom of the old courts of law. Although current practice is more practical for ferreting out the truth, nonetheless that old forum exercised eloquence more in which no one was compelled to plead his entire case in a very few hours and there were liberal adjournments and each orator imposed his own limits upon his address and the number of days or advocates was not defined. Gnaeus Pompey in his third consulship[58] was the first to confine these and, as it were, put reins upon eloquence, in such a way, nevertheless, that everything was carried on in the forum, in accordance with the laws, and before the praetors; to what extent the more important cases were customarily in times past tried before them is shown by nothing more clearly than that the cases pleaded before the court of one hundred,[59] which now hold the first rank of importance, were so eclipsed by the renown of the other courts that we do not read of the delivery of any speech of Cicero or Caesar or Brutus or Caelius or Calvus or, indeed, of any great orator before the hundred, with the exception of Asinius' speeches composed in behalf of Urbinia's heirs, and even these were delivered by Pollio in the middle of the reign of the deified Augustus, after a long period of peace and the people's continuous repose and the uninterrupted serenity of the senate and the very great statesmanship of the emperor had completely silenced eloquence itself as it had all things.

39. *The manner in which courts are now conducted hampers oratory.*

"What I am going to say will perhaps seem trivial and absurd, but I shall say it anyway, even if only that it may be laughed at. How much do we think that eloquence has been debased by those cloaks[60] in which, hampered and, as it were, bound up,

[57] See the beginning of book 2 of Lucretius' *On the Nature of Things*.
[58] When he was sole consul for almost the first half of the year 52 B.C.
[59] See footnote 6.
[60] In the old days, the toga was the proper dress for court appearance. It was

we chat with the judges? How much power do we believe has been stripped from a speech by auditoria and archive offices, in which nowadays the great majority of cases are generally disposed of? For, just as a spacious race track proves high-born steeds, so too there is a kind of testing ground for orators; unless they are borne through it free and unhampered, eloquence is weakened and then broken. Nay further, we know by experience that care and concern for preparation are harmful because often the judge asks a question before you begin and you have to take your point of departure from his question, and he frequently imposes silence on proof and evidence. In the midst of these things, one or at most two people stand by the speaker, and the case is carried on as if in a desert. However, the orator needs noise and applause and a kind of theater, as it were: such things were daily at the disposal of the ancient orators, when so many and such distinguished men packed the forum at the same time, when also clients and the members of tribes and even embassies of communities and part of Italy stood by those who were in danger, when in most cases the Roman people believed that it made a difference to them what the verdict was. It is beyond question that Gaius Cornelius and Marcus Scaurus and Titus Milo and Lucius Bestia and Publius Vatinius[61] were prosecuted and defended with the whole state there assembled, so that the very enthusiasms of the people in rivalry were able to arouse and set afire even the most phlegmatic orators. And indeed speeches of this kind survive, so that even the very men who delivered them are not more distinguished for any others.

40. *A well-ordered state does not produce great orators since they are not needed.*

"Then, indeed, what remarkable stimulus was furnished genius, what fire was given orators by the continual public gatherings and the privilege that was granted of attacking the most powerful men and the very glory of feuds, when very many good speakers did not keep from tangling even with Publius Scipio or Sulla or Gnaeus Pompey and, the nature of envy being what it is, used the ears of the people, just as actors do, to attack the leading men of the state.

---

later replaced by the *paenula*, a tight-fitting sleeveless cloak. The change was indicative of the loss of dignity suffered by the legal profession.

[61] These famous cases, in all of which Cicero spoke for the defense, occurred in the years between 65 and 52 B.C.

"We are not speaking about a calm and peaceful state, one which gets pleasure from uprightness and moderation, but that great and renowned eloquence is the offspring of license, which fools call liberty, the companion of seditions, the instigator of an unbridled people, without respect, without dignity, violent, rash, arrogant, which does not appear in well-governed states. Of what Lacedaemonian or Cretan orator have we heard? The constitutions and laws of these states are reported to have been most strict. We do not even know of eloquence among the Macedonians and Persians or any people who were satisfied with stable government. Certain orators appeared in Rhodes and very many at Athens, where the commons, the inexperienced, all men, so to speak, had all power. Our state too, as long as it wandered aimlessly, as long as it weakened itself by means of partisan politics and dissensions and discords, as long as there was no peace in the forum, no common policy in the senate, no self-restraint in the law courts, no respect for authority, no restrictions imposed by the magistrates, undoubtedly produced a more vigorous eloquence, just as an uncultivated field produces certain more luxuriant plants. But neither the eloquence of the Gracchi was of such great advantage to the state that the latter even put up with their laws nor did Cicero find oratorical renown adequate compensation for his terrible death.[62]

41. *Rome today is well governed by a wise emperor. Each age should therefore enjoy its own blessings.*

"Thus, too, the forum, which survives the ancient orators, is proof of a state not faultless or as well ordered as one could wish. For who calls upon us except the man guilty or miserable? What community comes into our protection unless either a neighboring people or internal disagreement is the cause? What province do we represent except one that has been plundered and despoiled? And yet it would have been better for no complaint to arise than for a complaint to be avenged. But if some state should be found in which no one did wrong, the orator would be unnecessary among guiltless people, as a doctor is among healthy ones. Just as, nonetheless, the doctor's skill has very little use and shows little progress among those nations which enjoy the best health and the soundest bodies, thus the

---

[62] Cicero was beheaded by Antony's henchmen near his villa at Formiae, on December 7, 43 B.C. See Juvenal, *Satires* 10. 118ff.

prestige of orators is less and their glory duller among people of high moral character who are ready to obey their ruler. For what need is there for long expressions of opinion in the senate when the best men quickly come to an agreement? What is the need for many meetings before the people, when the ignorant masses are not deciding a matter of public policy but the one individual who is the wisest? What is the need for prosecutions undertaken by individuals, when wrongdoing is so rarely and sparingly committed? What the need for defenses that produce enmity and go beyond all bounds, when the mercy of the judge embraces those in danger? You, gentlemen, who are excellent and most eloquent men, as far as the need exists, believe me, if you had been born in earlier centuries and those at whom we marvel in these, and some god had suddenly exchanged lives and times, you would not have lacked that very great praise and glory in eloquence, nor they moderation and a sense of proportion; now, since no one can attain great renown and great repose at the same time, let each one enjoy the blessing of his own age without detracting from the other."

42. *The gathering breaks up and all depart.*

Maternus finished, and then Messalla said: "There were some points with which I would disagree, there were others which I would like treated at greater length, except that the day is already far gone." Maternus responded, "We will do it whenever you wish in the future, and if some things seemed unclear to you in this discourse of mine, we shall consider them again." And, getting up at once and having embraced Aper, he said, "I shall make charges against you before the poets, while Messalla will do the same before the lovers of antiquity." "And I shall indict both of you before the rhetoricians and schoolmasters," said Aper.

When they had smiled, we departed.

Index

This index includes practically all appearances of proper names, in the introduction and footnotes as well as in the text of the translation. Titles of literary works are also listed. Excluded are the author's name, "Agricola," "Britain," and "British" in the *Agricola*, "Germany" and "Germans" in the *Germany*, and "Rome" and "Romans." Roman names are normally listed by *cognomina*, i.e., the last of the customary three parts of the nomenclature, although some Romans had names consisting of only two parts and some had names with four or more. The few exceptions are men well known in English by their *nomina*, such as Vergil and Horace.

The Oklahoma Series in Classical Culture is a publishing venture of the University of Oklahoma Press. The series formalizes the Press's long tradition of publishing books in the classical fields. Series editor A. J. Heisserer (University of Oklahoma) and an advisory board of twelve distinguished scholars from the United States, Canada, and Great Britain work closely with the University of Oklahoma Press to publish books of the highest quality in the following areas:

(1) General studies in ancient culture, including literature, history, and archaeology.

(2) General textbooks in English intended primarily for use in undergraduate courses.

(3) Classroom textbooks intended primarily for use in Greek and Latin courses, such books invariably containing the text in the original language together with helpful notes for students.

(4) Specialized monographs in ancient culture, dealing with such areas as ancient medicine, Ciceronian studies, Latin literature in the Late Empire, and the social and political history of Classical Greece.